English Reading

English Reading

© 이숙희, 2019
1판 1쇄 인쇄__2019년 12월 20일
1판 1쇄 발행__2019년 12월 30일

편저자__이숙희
펴낸이__홍정표
펴낸곳__글로벌콘텐츠
　　　　등록__제25100-2008-000024호
　　　　이메일__edit@gcbook.co.kr

공급처__(주)글로벌콘텐츠출판그룹
　　　　대표__홍정표 이사__김미미 편집__김봄 이예진 권군오 홍명지 기획·마케팅__노경민 이종훈
　　　　주소__서울특별시 강동구 풍성로 87-6(성내동) 전화__02) 488-3280 팩스__02) 488-3281
　　　　홈페이지__http://www.gcbook.co.kr

값 13,500원
ISBN 979-11-5852-268-1 13740

English
Reading

이숙희 편저

글로벌콘텐츠

Content

Essays

Stories

머리말

이 책은 대학 수준의 학습자를 위한 영어 독해 연습 책이다. 대학 수준의 학습자는 외국어로 된 글감이라도 그 내용에 있어서는 고급 수준을 기대한다. 이 책은 그런 학습자의 기대를 고려하여 내용을 최우선적으로 고려하여 구성하였다.

수록된 글은 크게 에세이와 단편소설 두 영역으로 나뉜다. 에세이 관련 글은 20대 학습자들의 삶과 연결될 수 있는 소재의 글들로 선별하였다. 미래로 나아가는 자세, 현실의 스트레스를 극복하는 방법, 다양한 문화와 목소리들에 대한 간접 경험 등이 에세이들의 주된 내용이다. 이러한 주제들이 고루하지 않고 생생한 시대적 감각으로 다뤄질 수 있도록 글감은 모두 동시대 작가의 것들도 골랐으며, 또한 20대 학습자가 주제에 대해 좀 더 긴밀한 친연성을 느낄 수 있도록 같은 연령대의 작가 글도 몇몇 포함시켰다.

단편소설은 에세이 보다 스타일이 다양하고 의미가 더 암시적일 수 있으므로 읽기의 난이도가 더 높다. 이 점을 고려하여 단편소설 영역에서는 다소 평이한 텍스트에서 시작하여 점점 고난도 텍스트로 이행하는 방식으로 작품을 배열하였다. 각 단편소설들은 상징, 복선, 플롯, 시점, 아이러니 등 문학의 기본적 요소도 잘 갖추고 있어서 언어 능력뿐만 아니라 문학적 감각도 함께 익힐 수 있을 것이다.

각 글들은 학습자가 충분히 자기 주도적 학습을 할 수 있도록 독해 교재 방식으로 구조화하였다. 우선 읽기 전 자료로 주요 단어 및 구절을 정리하였다. 학습자가 다소 기계적인 단어 및 구문 익힘을 사전에 완료함으로써 글 전체를 의미 중심으로 몰입하여 읽을 수 있도록 유도한 것이다. 또한 읽기 중간 단계에서도 내용 파악이 어려울 수 있는 부분이나 구문이 모호한 부분은 주석으로 정리하여 읽기가 유연하게 마지막까지 이어지도록 하였다. 읽기가 끝나면 읽기 후 활동으로 Comprehension Check-Up Questions를 부가하였다. 이 질문들은 모두 본문의 내용과 직접적으로 관련된 이른바 'skinny questions'들로서 그 답이 명시적으로 글 속에 드러나 있다. 이런 질문에 대해 답을 하면서 학습자는 자신의 주도적 읽기가 제대로 이루어졌는지 쉽게 점검할 수 있을 것이다. 질문에 대한 답이 모호한 경우 다시 해당 부분으로 옮겨 재독함으로써 글 전체에 대한 학습자의 자신감은 더 상승하게 된다.

이 책의 사용자가 고등 사고력을 가진 학습자이고 글감 또한 깊이 있는 내용임을 고려할 때 각 글에는 다양한 유추적 사고, 창의적 사고를 요구하는 이른바 'fat questions'이 포함되어야 한다고 생각할 수 있을 것이다. 그러나 학습자의 일차적 목표가 다양한 글감을 정확하게 이해하는 데에 있으므로 너무 많은 창의적 활동은 잘못하면 이 일차적 목표를 흐리게 할 위험도 있다. 이 책은 정확한 이해라는 읽기의 일차적 목표에 주력하기로 하여 읽기 후 활동에 토론 등 다른 활동을 포함하지 않았다. 교수자는 필요한 경우 자신의 수업에 맞는 창의 활동을 별도의 자료로 만들어 이 점을 보완할 수 있을 것이다.

Essays

A Different Drummer

Jonathan Baily

Jonathan Baily (1977) wrote the following essay as part of his admission application for Stanford University. The essay was reprinted in the university's alumni magazine.

Words and Phrases

tap	beckon
countertap	drive a punk quartet
throne	

I was born a little bit different from everyone else. I have no fingers, only a thumb, on my left hand. Throughout much of my life I was ashamed of my physical distinction.[1] I believed that people would judge my character based on what my hand looked like, and I feared rejection. One thing in particular helped to change my perspective[2]: the drums.

---

[1] my physical distinction: his physical difference without fingers on the left hand.
[2] my perspective: thinking that others reject him because of his physical difference.

When I was thirteen, as my stepmother and I stood in the kitchen talking, I began to tap on the table. My stepmother, who was once a musician, immediately noticed a good sense of rhythm in my countertapping endeavor and suggested we consider starting me on the drums.3)

I was surprised that she would even suggest such a thing. Drums required two hands and I had only one. However, the very next day, the two of us were off4) to the music store to purchase a pair of drumsticks and a "practice pad." Six months later we purchased my drum set.

I'll never forget the first time I sat on the throne of my new drum set. My entire body shook with excitement. I had always wanted to play the drums, but I never believed I could. I thought "my disability" would stop me. Now, before me lay not just one drum, but an entire drum set,5) beckoning me to play. I cautiously picked up my drumsticks and, ever so gently,6) began tapping on first one, and then all of the drums and cymbals. Then I let loose.7) I sounded awful, but I didn't care. It was one of the most romantic experiences of my life. Never had I been so enveloped in a blanket

---

3) suggested to consider starting me on the drum: mom suggested that we consider starting me on the drum. start는 여기서 타동사.

4) were off: went.

5) before me lay not just one drum, but an entire drum set: not just one drum but an entire drum set lay in front of me.

6) ever so gently: very gently.

7) let loose: got free: got relaxed.

of pulsating frequencies and tones.[8] I was in love. My parents, however, were not, and we quickly agreed that I could continue playing the drums only if I took lessons.[9] It was settled.[10] I started my lessons and began to practice.

Drums were not only a source of pleasure and joy for me, they became the means by which I realized that I could use my left hand productively. By being able to play the drums, I discovered that my left hand could be used to produce something beautiful, something useful, and I realized its unique importance. Instead of hating my hand, I began to respect it _ to respect me.

Through my drums, my hand and I have become one. Now, when I meet new people, I no longer fear that the first part of me a person sees will be my hand.[11] That person may see my heart, as I share with him a poem I have just finished. Another person will see my mind, as I discuss with her Newton's Law of Universal Gravitation. Another will see me, sitting behind the

---

8) Never had I been so enveloped in a blanket of pulsating frequencies and tones: 고동치는 박자와 음조에 그렇게 포근하게 쌓여본 경험이 없었다. blanket은 은유로서 담요처럼 자신을 포근하게 감싸는 듯한 frequencies and tones를 가리킴. 부정어귀 Never가 문장 앞에 와서 주어 동사의 위치 도치.

9) I could continue playing the drums only if I took lessons: 레슨을 받는 조건으로 드럼을 계속 칠 수 있도록 함.

10) It was settled: 그렇게 합의함으로써 문제 일단락됨.

11) the first part of me a person sees will be my hand: the first part of me/ a person sees/ will be my hand 누구를 만날 때 그 사람이 나의 모습 중 손을 제일 먼저 볼 것이라고 생각하는 것.

fruit of my passion, the drums,[12] driving a punk quartet or the school jazz band. And if that person does see my hand _ what of it?[13] It is with this hand that I make music.[14] It is with this hand that I write a poem, or do a calculus problem, or stroke a kitten. What more could I possibly want? I am complete.

---

12) fruit of my passion, the drums: fruit of my passion = the drums.
13) what of it?: it's no problem.
14) It is with this hand that I make music: It. . .that. . . 강조 용법.

Comprehension Check-Up Questions

1. What does the writer mean by "physical distinction"?

2. How was his talent found out?

3. What expressions reveal his excitement when he first got his drum set?

4. Drums were not just music instruments for the narrator but contributed a lot for his self esteem. Explain how.

5. How does the last paragraph show the writer's gender sensitivity?

Who Controls Your Life?

Charles G. Russell and Judith White

Charles G. Russell (b. L937), professor of communication at the University of Toledo in Ohio and a consultant in management and communications, and Judith White (b. 1946) is president of Scribe communications, a writing and editing service based in Ann Arbor, Michigan, argue that one should hold the ownership of feeling.

Words and Phrases	
attribute	
causality	heated argument
relieve A of B	pervasive
assert/assertion	linguistic cop-out
inadvertently	ascribe

"He made me angry!", "She makes me feel stupid." Feeling angry and stupid and attributing the cause of the feelings to someone else relieves us of the responsibility for our feelings.[1] If others can control when and if we feel angry, happy, stupid,

---

1) 문장의 동사는 relieves. relieve ~ of ~.

or anything else, they, in effect, control our lives. The words "make" and "made" can play a significant role in our feeling powerless to control our feelings. As long as we accept, without question, the power of others to determine our feelings, we perhaps abandon any chance of controlling our own lives.

When we attribute causality for our feelings with the "make" and "made", we assert that something we feel or experience happens[2] because someone else makes it happen. If this assertion were accurate, we could not change whatever we experience or feel, unless the other person permitted the change. Yet the feelings change dramatically from angry to amused[3] without others giving permission to change our feelings. Think about the last time you had a "heated argument" with someone and felt very angry until someone else walked into the room.[4] Did the other person give you permission to stop feeling angry on your own?

No doubt you recognize that you had the power to feel any way you wanted and that the other person could not really force you to feel anything you did not allow yourself to feel.[5] Even with any recognition that we really can control our own feelings, the words

---

2) something we feel or experience/ happens.
3) from angry to amused 화난 상태에서 기쁜 상태로. angry와 amused 앞에 being 생략.
4) Think about the last time// you had a "heated argument" with someone and felt very angry/until someone else walked into the room.
5) No doubt/ you recognize// that you had the power to feel any way you wanted/ and that the other person could not really force you to feel anything/ you did not allow yourself to feel.

"make" or "made" continue to dominate our conversations. If you were to count the numbers you and others attribute the responsibility for feelings to someone else,[6] you will discover the pervasive nature of those words in our conversations.

The words "make" and "made" can easily contribute to our forgetting that we, and not others, control our feelings.[7] As long as we assign responsibility for choices we make to others, we'll continue doing so, even if these choices do not serve us well. Thinking that others "cause" our feelings relieves us of assuming responsibilities or choices we make.[8] This "linguistic cop-out" ensures that we will continue to allow others to control our lives.[9] If you want to ensure control over your own feelings, you can begin by not using the words "make" and "made". ⋯⋯ Do we really want to accept responsibility for our feelings? If we do, our use of the words "make" and "made" will probably diminish. If we do not want to claim responsibility for our feelings, we can continue to declare "You made me feel stupid!"

---

6) If you were to count the numbers/ you and others attribute the responsibility for feelings to someone else, 가정법 문장. were to는 일어날 확률이 없는 현재 사실에 대한 가정법 동사형.

7) our forgetting that we, and not others, control our feelings. 다른 사람이 아니라 우리가 우리 자신의 감정을 컨트롤한다는 사실을 잊어버림. that 이하는 forgetting의 목적절.

8) Thinking that others "cause" our feelings// relieves us of assuming responsibilities or choices/ we make. 다른 사람이 우리 감정을 유발한다고 생각하는 것은 우리가 하는 결정에 대한 책임을 우리 스스로 떠맡지 않도록 해준다. 즉 다른 사람에게 감정 유발 책임을 돌림으로써 자신이 책임져야 할 감정 컨트롤 역할을 피하려고 함.

9) This "linguistic cop-out"/ ensures/ that we will continue to allow others to control our lives.

Comprehension Check-Up Questions

1. According to the authors, why is it dangerous to frequently use the words "make" and "made"?

2. In what ways can we find out how inadvertently we use those words in our daily basis?

3. What do the authors suggest for us to keep the ownership of our feelings?

Steve Job's Stanford Commencement Speech

Steve Jobs

A commencement speech or commencement address is a speech given to graduating students, generally at a university, generally in the United States, although the term is also used for secondary education institutions. The "commencement" is a ceremony in which degrees or diplomas are conferred upon graduating students. A commencement speech is typically given by a notable figure in the community, during the commencement exercise. The person giving such a speech is known as a commencement speaker. Very commonly, colleges or universities will invite politicians, important citizens, or other noted speakers to come and address the graduating class. A commencement speech is less bound by the structure found in other forms of public address, like eulogies or wedding speeches. The speaker accordingly enjoys a unique freedom to express him or herself. The following commencement speech was made by Steve Jobs in 2005 for Stanford University graduates and is known as one of the most notable commencement speeches in the U.S..

Words and Phrases

commencement(n.): beginning; drop: fall, give up; quit

drop-in

biological mother

a young, unwed college graduate student

adoption

except that

pop out

relent

working-class parents' savings

college tuition

stumbled into

curiosity and intuition

priceless

calligraphy: Calli ("beauty") + graphy "to write"

life hits you in the head with a brick

many days in a row

diagnosed with cancer

serif and san serif typefaces

typography

subtle: delicate

practical application

proportionally spaced fonts

turned 30

diverge

side with sb

publically out

entrepreneur

let down: To fail to meet the expectations of; disappoint.

screw up

the valley: Sillicon Valley

computer animated feature film

current renaissance

microscope

the single best invention of Life

trapped by dogma

drown out your inner voice

tumor on my pancreas	The Whole Earth Catalog
incurable	final issue
be buttoned up	back cover
diagnosis	
intestines	

I

Thank you. I'm honored to be with you today for your commencement from one of the finest universities in the world. Truth be told, I never graduated from college and this is the closest I've ever gotten to a college graduation.

Today I want to tell you three stories from my life. That's it. No big deal. Just three stories. The first story is about connecting the dots.

I dropped out of Reed College after the first six months but then stayed around as a drop-in for another eighteen months or so before I really quit. So why did I drop out? It started before I was born. My biological mother was a young, unwed graduate student, and she decided to put me up for adoption. She felt very strongly that I should be adopted by college graduates, so everything was all set for me to be adopted at birth by a lawyer and his wife, except that when I popped out, they decided at the last minute that they really wanted a girl. So my parents, who were on a waiting list, got a call in the middle of the night asking, "We've got an unexpected baby boy. Do you want him?" They said, "Of course." My biological mother found out later that my mother had never graduated from college and that my father had never graduated from high school. She refused to sign the final adoption papers. She only relented a few months later when my parents promised that I would go to college.

This was the start in my life. And seventeen years later, I did go to college, but I naively chose a college that was almost as expensive as Stanford, and all of my working-class parents' savings were being spent on my college tuition. After six months, I couldn't see the value in it. I had no idea what I wanted to do with my life, and no idea of how college was going to help me figure it out, and here I was, spending all the money my parents had saved their entire life.[1] So I decided to drop out and trust that it would all work out OK.[2] It was pretty scary at the time, but looking back, it was one of the best decisions I ever made.[3] The minute I dropped out,[4] I could

---

1) no idea how college was going to help me figure it out: I had no idea how college was going to help me figure it out. It= what I wanted to do with my life.
2) trust that it would all work out OK: I trust that it would all work out OK: it = dropping out.
3) looking back it was one of the best decisions I ever made: looking back 지금 와서 돌아보면. (분사구문)

stop taking the required classes that didn't interest me and begin dropping in on the ones that looked far more interesting.

It wasn't all romantic. I didn't have a dorm room, so I slept on the floor in friends' rooms. I returned Coke bottles for the five-cent deposits to buy food with, and I would walk the seven miles across town every Sunday night to get one good meal a week at the Hare Krishna temple. I loved it. And much of what I stumbled into by following my curiosity and intuition turned out to be priceless later on.[5] Let me give you one example.

Reed College at that time offered perhaps the best calligraphy instruction in the country. Throughout the campus every poster, every label on every drawer was beautifully hand-calligraphed.[6] Because I had dropped out and didn't have to take the normal classes, I decided to take a calligraphy class to learn how to do this. I learned about serif and sans-serif typefaces, about varying the amount of space between different letter combinations, about what makes great typography great. It was beautiful, historical, artistically subtle in a way that science can't capture, and I found it fascinating.

None of this had even a hope of any practical application in

---

4) The minute I dropped out: as soon as I dropped out.

5) much of what I stumbled into by following my curiosity and intuition/ turned out/ to be priceless later on.

6) Throughout the campus/ every poster, every label on every drawer,/ was beautifully hand calligraphed: every는 단수 취급이므로 동사 역시 was.

my life. But ten years later when we were designing the first Macintosh computer, it all came back to me, and we designed it all into the Mac. It was the first computer with beautiful typography. If I had never dropped in on that single course in college, the Mac would have never had multiple typefaces or proportionally spaced fonts,[7] and since Windows just copied the Mac, it's likely that no personal computer would have them.

If I had never dropped out, I would have never dropped in on that calligraphy class and personals computers might not have the wonderful typography that they do.

Of course it was impossible to connect the dots looking forward when I was in college, but it was very, very clear looking backwards 10 years later. Again, you can't connect the dots looking forward. You can only connect them looking backwards, so you have to trust that the dots will somehow connect in your future. You have to trust in something — your gut, destiny, life, karma, whatever — because believing that the dots will connect down the road will give you the confidence to follow your heart, even when it leads you off the well-worn path, and that will make all the difference.

---

7) If I had never dropped in on that single course in college, the Mac would have never had multiple typefaces or proportionally spaced fonts: single course=calligraphy class. 가정법에 유의. 이하 많은 문장들이 가정법.

II

My second story is about love and loss. I was lucky. I found what I loved to do early in life. Woz and I started Apple in my parents' garage when I was twenty. We worked hard and in ten years, Apple had grown from just the two of us in a garage into a $2 billion company with over 4,000 employees. We'd just released our finest creation, the Macintosh, a year earlier, and I'd just turned thirty, and then I got fired. How can you get fired from a company you started? Well, as Apple grew, we hired someone who I thought was very talented to run the company with me, and for the first year or so, things went well.[8] But then our visions of the future began to diverge, and eventually we had a falling out. When we did, our board of directors sided with him, and so at thirty, I was out, and very publicly out. What had been the focus of my entire adult life was gone[9], and it was devastating. I really didn't know what to do for a few months. I felt that I had let the previous generation of entrepreneurs down, that I had dropped the baton as it was being passed to me. I met with David Packard and Bob Noyce and tried to apologize for screwing up so badly. I was a very public failure and I even thought about running away from the

---

8) Well, as Apple grew/ we hired someone who (I thought) was very talented to run the company with me, and for the first year or so/ things went well.
9) What had been the focus of my entire adult life/ was gone.

Valley. But something slowly began to dawn on me. I still loved what I did. The turn of events at Apple had not changed that one bit. I'd been rejected but I was still in love. And so I decided to start over.

I didn't see it then, but it turned out that getting fired from Apple was the best thing that could have ever happened to me. The heaviness of being successful was replaced by the lightness of being a beginner again, less sure about everything. It freed me to enter one of the most creative periods in my life. During the next five years I started a company named NeXT, another company named Pixar and fell in love with an amazing woman who would become my wife. Pixar went on to create the world's first computer-animated feature film, "Toy Story", and is now the most successful animation studio in the world.

In a remarkable turn of events, Apple bought NeXT and I returned to Apple and the technology we developed at NeXT is at the heart of Apple's current renaissance, and Lorene and I have a wonderful family together.

I'm pretty sure none of this would have happened if I hadn't been fired from Apple. It was awful-tasting medicine but I guess the patient needed it. Sometimes life's going to hit you in the head with a brick. Don't lose faith. I'm convinced that the only thing that kept me going was that I loved what I did. You've got to find what you love, and that is as true for work as it is for your lovers. Your work is going to fill a large part of your life, and the only way to be truly satisfied is to do what you believe is great work, and the only way to do great work is to love what you do. If you haven't found it yet, keep looking, and don't settle. As with all matters of the heart, you'll know when you find it, and like any great relationship it just gets better and better as the years roll on. So keep looking. Don't settle.

III

My third story is about death. When I was 17 I read a quote that went something like "If you live each day as if it was your last, someday you'll most certainly be right." It made an impression on me, and since then, for the past 33 years, I have looked in the mirror every morning and asked myself, "If today were the last day of my life, would I want to do what I am about to do today?" And whenever the answer has been "no" for too many days in a row, I know I need to change something. Remembering that I'll be dead soon is the most important thing I've ever encountered to help me make the big choices in life, because almost everything — all external expectations, all pride, all fear of embarrassment or failure — these things just fall away in the face of death, leaving only what is truly important.

Remembering that you are going to die is the best way I know to avoid the trap of thinking you have something to lose.[10) You are already naked. There is no reason not to follow your heart.

About a year ago, I was diagnosed with cancer. I had a scan at 7:30 in the morning and it clearly showed a tumor on my pancreas. I didn't even know what a pancreas was. The doctors told me this was almost certainly a type of cancer that is incurable, and that I should expect to live no longer than three to six months. My doctor advised me to go home and get my affairs in order, which is doctors' code for "prepare to die."[11) It means to try and tell your kids everything you thought you'd have the next ten years to tell them, in just a few months. It means to make sure that everything is buttoned up so that it will be as easy as possible for your family. It means to say your goodbyes.

I lived with that diagnosis all day. Later that evening I had a biopsy where they stuck an endoscope down my throat, through my stomach into my intestines, put a needle into my pancreas and got a few cells from the tumor. I was sedated but my wife, who was there, told me that when they viewed the cells under a microscope, the doctor started crying, because it turned out to be a very rare form of pancreatic cancer that is curable with surgery. I had the surgery and, thankfully, I am fine now.

---

10) Remembering that you are going to die/ is/ the best way (I know) to avoid the trap of thinking you have something to lose.
11) which is doctor's code for prepare to die: 앞 문장 전체를 받는 which.

This was the closest I've been to facing death, and I hope it's the closest I get for a few more decades. Having lived through it, I can now say this to you with a bit more certainty than when death was a useful but purely intellectual concept. No one wants to die, even people who want to go to Heaven don't want to die to get there, and yet, death is the destination we all share. No one has ever escaped it. And that is as it should be, because death is very likely the single best invention of life. It's life's change agent; it clears out the old to make way for the new. Right now, the new is you. But someday, not too long from now, you will gradually become the old and be cleared away. Sorry to be so dramatic, but it's quite true. Your time is limited, so don't waste it living someone else's life. Don't be trapped by dogma, which is living with the results of other people's thinking. Don't let the noise of others' opinions drown out your own inner voice, heart and intuition. They somehow already know what you truly want to become. Everything else is secondary.

When I was young, there was an amazing publication called *The Whole Earth Catalogue*, which was one of the bibles of my generation. It was created by a fellow named Stuart Brand not far from here in Menlo Park, and he brought it to life with his poetic touch. This was in the late Sixties, before personal computers and desktop publishing, so it was all made with typewriters, scissors, and Polaroid cameras. it was sort of like

Google in paperback form thirty-five years before Google came along. I was idealistic, overflowing with neat tools and great notions. Stuart and his team put out several issues of the *The Whole Earth Catalogue*, and then when it had run its course, they put out a final issue.[12] It was the mid-Seventies and I was your age. On the back cover of their final issue was a photograph of an early morning country road, the kind you might find yourself hitchhiking on if you were so adventurous. Beneath were the words, "Stay hungry, stay foolish." It was their farewell message as they signed off. "Stay hungry, stay foolish." And I have always wished that for myself, and now, as you graduate to begin anew, I wish that for you. Stay hungry, stay foolish. Thank you all, very much.

---

12) when it had run its course, they put out a final issue: 전 과정을 마치고 마침내 최종판 을 냈다.

1. In what process was Jobs adopted?

2. Why did Jobs drop out the college?

3. What is the lesson of Jobs' first story?

4. When and where did Jobs start Apple company?

5. How did he get fired from Apple and how much did he suffer from it?

6. What unexpected effects did he get after his "public failure" of being out?

7. What is the lesson of Jobs' second story?

8. What illness did Jobs undergo and how long was he expected to live?

9. How did his cancer turn out after biopsy?

10. Why does Jobs think death is the best invention of Life?

11. What is the lesson of Jobs' last story?

Dress as Success:
Interview with Joolz

Wendy Chapkis

Wendy Chapkis is currently professor of sociology and women and gender studies, University of Southern Maine.Wendy Chapkis engages in research and teaching on such issues as drug policy reform, LGBTQ history and culture, body politics, and inequalities/intersections of gender, race, nationality, and class. She is also the author of three books: *Beauty Secrets: Women and the Politics of Appearance (1986);* *Live Sex Acts: Women Performing Erotic Labor (1997); and Dying to Get High: Marijuana as Medicine* (with Richard J. Webb; 2008). In her book *Beauty Secrets: Women and the Politics of Appearance*, from which the following selection is taken, Chapkis writes of how cultural ideals of beauty are passed on to us through film, advertising, and even self-help books. The book also includes interviews with women who do not fit the normal idea of beauty. Joolz's interview that follows is one example of them.

Words and Phrases

outrageous looking

the heavy metal image

under the circumstances

domestic

insecure

reassuring

restrictive

go down well

dye

bleach

shocking pink

fluorescent green

fire Red

puppet

mermaid

have something to do with

statement

constricting

constricting

stage costume

lycra and sequins

take after

more presentable

adolescent

insecure

hideous

glam

anarchy

nerve

relative

pierced nose

tattoo/tattooist

celtic style

for a giggle

wig

tremendous: fantastic

relieved

sexist

walk all over you

stare

rarely

make contact

feather boas	license
fans	straight looks
studs	afford to
appeal to ~	look ragged
tiresome	failure of nerve
confuse the eye	have my hair done
straight away	salon
venue	suburbs
sound crew	row of ladies
security men	tremendously
to be messed with	get sick of
	tempting

I

I was nineteen when I married a man who became a Satan's Slave. During the time I was with him, I looked pretty normal. Bikers don't like outrageous looking girls at all. They do like "nice-looking" girls, though. And they prefer it if you have long hair. It fits with the heavy metal image.

You aren't to wear too much make-up or anything like that, and you wear jeans or trousers because you are on the bike so much. Though some of the girls did wear miniskirts which I always thought pretty stupid under the circumstances. The men clearly liked very girly girls. Oh, and they preferred blondes!

I never paid too much attention to how I was supposed to look.[1] I wore my hair short. It was more comfortable under the helmet. And I used to walk around in boy's clothes all the time. It was a bit of a problem for my husband in the club.[2] But eventually they accepted me because they decided I was artistic and if I was an artist I was allowed to be eccentric. In general, the women were expected to be very domestic and they were.

The club is a close tribal community. Because my background had been so insecure, I found it very reassuring in the beginning. But after five years, I left. It had become too restrictive.

Even before I left my husband, I already had become interested in the punk image. I had already dyed my hair pink _ something which didn't go down well in the club.

To dye your hair this color, you've got to first bleach it absolutely white, to strip it right down to the roots. I've had it this way for four years now. Pink was an easy first choice; it was a fashionable color, if you remember. Shocking pink and fluorescent

---

1) how I was supposed to look 내가 어떻게 보여야 하는가. be supposed to: should.
2) club: Satan's Slave club.

green, those were the colors associated with punk. Nowadays, I have it colored a bright scarlet, Fire Red.

II

Even when I was a child I wanted colored hair. I remember wanting waist-length green hair because there was this puppet in a children's show on television, a mermaid who never spoke but was extremely beautiful and had long green hair.

I've always tended toward fantasy[3], the fantastic. In fact my image may have more to do with fantasy than punk in the pure sense. Punk started off anti-fashion. So you set out to make yourself look as anti-pretty as possible. But I've always been too insecure to do it properly. I worry too much about what I actually look like.

My mother is very beautiful — feminine, small and pretty in the magazine style. I take after my father who is big. When I was a child, my mother was very disappointed in me and was always trying to make me more presentable. Other people's mothers used to shout at them for wearing make-up; my mother used to shout at me for not wearing any.[4]

When I was an adolescent, I suffered very badly from acne.

---

3) 나는 항상 fantasy 쪽으로 기우는 경향이 있었다.
4) any: any make-up.

I was also overweight. So I was sort of a tall, fat, spotty teenager. I had good teeth, though. My mother used to tell me "you have good teeth; smile, it's your best feature."

Having been a hideous adolescent, I've always been too insecure to intentionally make myself more hideous. I tend to sort of go to the "glam" side of punk rather than the anarchy. I always wanted a Mohican, but I never quite had the nerve to shave my head. I did have very, very short hair at one point, and I looked like a dog. And being big as well I was mistaken for a boy all the time. There are lots of things I wish I had the nerve to do with myself, but I just can't.

It's relative, of course. I imagine the way I look appears pretty outrageous to other people. Something like having a pierced nose I don't even think about anymore. But a lot of people seem to find it shocking.

My tattoos draw a lot of attention, too. I got tattooed for the first time when I was about nineteen. I had one on my wrist and another around my ankles. I thought they were alright at the time __ a sort of bracelet of flowers. But I only recently met a really good tattooist and have had new tattoos done over the old ones. These are in the Celtic style and are much better and much more extensive. Tattoos and tattooing fascinate me.

There are moments, though, when you get tired of it all. Everybody who looks this different feels that ways[5] sometimes,

5) that ways: you get tired of it all.

even if they don't admit it. There are mornings when I wake up and know I have to go down to the shops and wish that I looked like a perfectly ordinary person. But they[6] are not often enough for me to want to change anything.

Not too long ago, for a giggle, I borrowed a plain brown wig off a friend and put it on. It looked pretty convincing. I didn't put on much make-up and went to a gig that way. People who have known me for months and months didn't recognize me.

It was tremendous. But after a while, I didn't find it tremendous at all. I found it extremely unpleasant. I actually entered a state of panic. I was so relieved to take the wig off and be myself again.[7] I felt I had lost my whole personality. My whole statement was gone and I really hated it.[8]

The tattoos are the big thing actually. The scarlet hair you can just cut off if you get tired of it. But when you take the step of having big tattoos so close to the hands, you really make a permanent statement, especially as a woman.

---

6) they: are mornings when I wake up and know I have to go down to the shops and wish that I looked like a perfectly ordinary person.

7) 가발을 벗고 다시 나 자신이 되어서 마음이 편해졌다.

8) 나에 대한 표명(statement: 내가 이런 사람이다 라는 표현)이 [가발을 쓸 때] 사라져버렸고 나는 그런 사실이 싫었다.

III

I always wear long skirts and I always wear black. I don't wear jeans anymore because I wore them for so long when I was biking that I just got sick of them. They feel constricting to me.

Despite all the black and the tattoos and the skull rings, some of my stage costumes, made of lycra and sequins, are extremely glam. I love feather boas and fans. But always with studs; say[9] a studded belt at the waist. It is the combination that appeals to me. To be too completely glam would be tiresome. I like to confuse the eye.

The most important statement I am making through what I look like is one of strength. I have a strong personality and want to indicate that[10] straight away. Especially in the business I am in, it is important to have a strong image. Not just from the point of selling your records, but more importantly so that from the moment you walk into a venue you are noticed by the sound crew, the security men, everyone. They've got to know right away you are not someone to be messed with. This is particularly true for a woman. The rock business is totally sexist. If you are not a strong person, they will walk all over you.

---

9) say: for example.
10) that: I have a strong personality.

Of course sometimes the way I look frightens people. I was taking a train recently that was absolutely full __ people were standing in the corridors — and there was an empty seat next to me but nobody would sit in it. People will often stare, but they don't want to get too close and only rarely will they try to make contact.

Sometimes it seems that people feel that if you look "odd" it is a license for them to abuse you or threaten you[11]; it's as if the normal rules of politeness in society don't apply anymore.[12] You've given up straight looks, therefore you've given up any right to be treated with respect.

IV

A lot of people, particularly middle class people, look at punk and think it is a working class thing. But actually there are few working class punk rockers.[13] Only children of the middle class can afford to look ragged. It is a class statement, but not in the way people tend to assume. Punks are rejecting their class

---

11) people feel that if you look "odd" it is a license for them to abuse you or threaten you 사람들은 외모가 'odd'하면 쉽게 abuse 해버리거나 threaten 해버려도 된다고 생각한다. 그럴 권리(license)를 가진 것처럼.
12) [이 경우] 예의라는 일반적 룰이 더 이상 적용되지 않는 것처럼 보인다.
13) working class 출신의 로커는 거의 없다. 부정의 뜻을 가진 few에 주의할 것.

position, but you have to be there before you can reject it. Rejecting everything that's expected of you is not easy.

It is, in fact, very difficult to actually put yourself outside of society; to appear so different that you are beyond the normal relationships most women have.[14] I don't blame girls who are secretaries during the day and backcomb their hair a bit at night to come to the clubs. For those girls, punk is just fashion.

In a way, I am jealous of them[15] because, in the end, they can become normal. They can submerge themselves in the great stream of weddings and tumble dryers. But I also think that, somewhere inside them, they're disappointed. They know they have experienced a failure of nerve.[16]

I have my hair done by a woman named Lorraine. She works in a very small salon in the suburbs. Every time I go in there, I see this row of ladies with The Perm under the dryers just having had The Cut.[17] I once asked Lorraine "don't you ever get tremendously sick of doing this?" And she said "If another woman comes in who wants that Perm I'll scream and go mad!" But of course she'd then go and start rolling up the next woman's hair. The clients watch her working on me and they

---

14) to appear so different that you are beyond the normal relationships most women have 너무 다르게 보여서 대부분의 여성들이 갖는 정상적 관계 밖에 있는 듯이 보임. so that 용법.
15) them: [바로 앞에서 기술한] 낮에는 사무실에서 일하고 밤에는 펑크스타일로 클럽에 가는 여성들.
16) 이 문단에서 they는 모두 위 주석이 가리키는 여성들임.
17) 막 컷을 끝내고 드라이기 아래 앉아 펌을 하는 여성들. 즉 모든 미용실 여성들이 똑같은 헤어스타일을 한다는 뜻.

are fascinated. They'll come over and feel my hair and ask questions. It must be tremendously tempting for them to say "the hell with it; make mine scarlet too!"[18]

---

18) 그들은 "세상에! 내 머리도 진홍색으로 해주세요."라고 말하고 싶은 충동을 느낄 것이다.

Comprehension Check-Up Questions

1. Who are the interviewer and interviewee of the selection?

2. How was Joolz' style in the time of Satan's Slave club? How different was it from her associate girls and how did it provoke the male members?

3. From when was Joolz interested in dying hair? What dying style did she want and what motivated it?

4. Joolz categorizes her style rather as fantasy than punk. What is the difference between them and why does she prefer the former to the latter?

5. How did Joolz' preference of tatoos change? How often does she feel sick of her style including tatoos? Is it often enough for her to decide to give up her style?

6. Why is tatooing the big thing? In what aspects is it different from dying hair?

7. Describe Joolz' stage costumes as a combination style of punk and glam. Why does she like to combine the styles?

8. What does she consider most important regarding her style as an image and why?

9. Are many punks from working class? Why or why not?

10. Why is Joolz jealous of the girls who carry out normal lives during the day and enjoy punk style as well when necessary? Does she want to be one of them? Why or why not?

A Blizzard Under Blue Sky

Pam Houston

Pam Houston (born January 9, 1962 in Trenton, New Jersey) is an American author of short stories, novels and essays. She is best known for her first book, *Cowboys Are My Weakness* (1992), which has been translated into nine languages, and which won the 1993 Western States Book Award. Also, it was named a New York Times Notable Book in 1992. Houston's stories have been selected for volumes of Best American Short Stories. Major themes in Houston's work include relationships between men and women, the outdoors, animals and childhood trauma. She currently teaches in the MFA program at U.C. Davis, and at the Institute for American Indian Arts in Santa Fe. She directs the nonprofit Writing By Writers which puts on non-university based writing conferences across the American West and in France. Houston currently lives on a ranch at 9,000' above sea level in Colorado, near the headwaters of the Rio Grande River.

run rampant

inversion-clocked

salt lake city

city dwellers

ex: ex-girlfriend

alaska clipper

weather forecast

housemate

camper

kool-aid

bivvy sack

lighting paste

your butt

uncertain: not clear

clarity

precision

dried apricots

carnation

adjust a backpack

pack: backpack

trail

dip past twenty below zero

still air

lungs

fill up halfway

whines and whimpers

oversized

sheepdog-and-something-else

shatter glass

all grace

constant indecision

sneak rides on my skies

inventory: vt. check

thermarest

stove

flashlight

get chilled

mountain House

pleased with accomplishments

the sun slipped away

dusk came

super-metabolizer

couch potato

whine and wriggle

crystal palace

leap out of ~

moab

utah

fourth dimension

subzero weather

perception

sun crawling higher

minimal noise

intrude

brass band

squeaking

binding

slosh

whoosh

jangle

bass line and percussion

primal song

thump the snow

crystal-coated

diamond-studded

stop being simply white

stuff her entire body

full-length adj.

fear crept into my spine

cuddle

chastise

wonder Woman

risk vt.

numbness

crawling up

doze off

come back to senses

extremities

convince vt.

poke my head out of ~

down and nylon

rebirth of fingers and toes

two-stop

pack up vi.

something resembling glee

everest

iditarod: the annual 1,200-mile

alaske dog

translucent	supervise
snow cave	sled race
bank	antarctica
gentle slope	swirl
fatality	snowflake

I

The doctor said I was clinically depressed.[1] It was February, the month in which depression runs rampant in the inversion-cloaked Salt Lake Valley[2] and the city dwellers escape to Park City, where the snow is fresh and the sun is shining and everybody is happy, except me. In truth, my life was on the verge of more spectacular and satisfying discoveries than I had ever imagined, but of course I couldn't see that far ahead. What I saw was work that wasn't getting done, bills that weren't getting paid, and a man I'd given my heart to weekending in the desert with his ex.

The doctor said, "I can give you drugs." I said, "No way."

She said, "The machine that drives you is broken. You need something to help you get it fixed." I said, "Winter camping."

---

1) clinically depressed 의학적으로 우울증이다.
2) inversion은 대기의 위층이 온도가 높아서 먼지나 안개 등이 아래 (예: Salt Lake City 같은 도시)에 몰려 있는 상황. 즉 위는 맑으나 아래 부분에 구름 혹은 눈이 오는 상황.

She said, "Whatever floats your boat."[3] One of the things that I love the most about natural world is the way it gives you what's good for you even if you don't know it at the time. I had never been winter camping before, at least not in the high country, and the weekend I chose to try and fix my machine[4] was the same weekend the air mass they called the Alaska Clipper showed up.[5]

It was thirty-two degrees below zero in town on the night I spent in my snow cave. I don't know how cold it was out on Beaver Creek. I had listened to the weather forecast, and to the advice of my housemate, Alex, who was an experienced winter camper.

"I don't know what you think you're going to prove by freezing to death." Alex said, "but if you've got to go, take my bivvy sack; it's warmer than anything you have." "Thanks." I said.

"If you mix Kool-Aid with your water it won't freeze up" he said, "and don't forget lighting paste for your stove." "Okay." I said.

"I hope it turns out to be worth it." he said, "because you are going to freeze your butt."

---

3) 너의 보트가 가라앉지 않고 유지하도록 하는 것이면 무엇이든지. 즉 우울증에 빠지지 않고 일상생활을 할 수 있도록 하는 것이라면 '겨울 캠핑' 같은 것도 좋다.

4) 앞에 의사가 표현한 'machine': 너의 마음.

5) I had never been winter camping before, at least not in the high country, and the weekend I chose to try and fix my machine was the same weekend the air mass they called the Alaska Clipper showed up. 겨울철 캠핑을 해 본 적 없음, 적어도 산악 지대 (high country)에서의 겨울 캠핑은 해 본 적 없음. 내 기계(앞서 나온 기계, 나를 이끌어가는 기계, 즉 이 기계가 고장 났기 때문에 우울증)를 고치기로 한 주말(즉, 겨울 캠핑 가기로 한 날)에 공교롭게 알라스카 기단이 형성.

II

When everything in your life is uncertain, there's nothing quite like the clarity and precision of fresh snow and blue sky. That was the first thought I had on Saturday morning as I stepped away from the warmth of my truck and let my skis slap the snow in front of me. There was no wind and no clouds that morning, just still air and cold sunshine. The hair in my nostrils froze almost immediately. When I took a deep breath, my lungs only filled up halfway.

I opened the tailgate to excited whines and whimpers. I never go skiing without Jackson and Hailey: my two best friends, my yin and yang of dogs. Some of you might know Jackson. He's the oversized sheepdog-and-something-else with the great big nose and the bark that will shatter glass. He gets out and about more than I do. People I've never seen before come by my house daily and call him by name. He's all grace, and he's tireless; he won't go skiing with me unless I let him lead.[6] Hailey is not so graceful, and her body seems in constant indecision when she runs. When we ski she stays behind me, and on the downhills she tries to sneak rides on my skis.

The dogs ran circles in the chest-high snow while I inventoried

---

6) he won't go skiing with me unless I let him lead. 스키 타러 갈 때마다 Jackson은 내 앞에 가려 한다.

my backpack one more time to make sure I had everything I needed. My sleeping bag, my Thermarest, my stove, Alex's bivvy sack, matches, lighting paste, flashlight, knife. I brought three pairs of long underwear _ tops and bottoms _ so I could change once before I went to bed, and once again in the morning, so I wouldn't get chilled by my own sweat. I brought paper and pen, and Kool-Aid to mix with my water. I brought Montana House chicken stew and some freeze-dried peas, some peanut butter and honey, lots of dried apricots, coffee and Carnation instant breakfast for morning.

Jackson stood very still while I adjusted his backpack. He carries the dog food and enough water for all of us. He takes himself very seriously when he's got his pack on. He won't step off the trail for any reason, not even to chase rabbits, and he gets nervous and angry if I do. That morning he was impatient with me. "Miles to go, Mom." he said over his shoulder. I snapped my boots into my skis and we were off.7)

There are not too many good things you can say about temperatures that dip past twenty below zero, except this: They turn the landscape into a crystal palace and they turn your vision into Superman's. In the cold thin morning air the trees and mountains, even the twigs and shadows, seemed to leap out of the background like a 3-D movie, only it was better than

---

7) snapped my boots into my skies 스키 신발(boots)을 스키에 찰칵 하고 끼워 넣다.

3-D because I could feel the sharpness of the air. I have a friend in Moab who swears that Utah is the center of the fourth dimension, and although I know he has in mind something much different and more complicated than subzero weather, it was there, on that ice-edged morning, that I felt on the verge of seeing something more than depth perception in the brutal clarity of the morning sun.

As I kicked along the first couple of miles, I noticed the sun crawling higher in the sky and yet the day wasn't really warming, and I wondered if I should have brought another vest, another layer to put between me and the cold night ahead. It was utterly quiet out there, and what minimal noise we made intruded on the morning like a brass band: the squeaking of my bindings, the slosh of the water in Jackson's pack, the whoosh of nylon, the jangle of dog tags. It was the bass line and percussion to some primal song, and I kept wanting to sing to it, but I didn't know the words.

Jackson and I crested the top of a hill[8] and stopped to wait for Hailey. The trail stretched out as far as we could see into the meadow below us and beyond.

"Nice place." I said to Jackson, and his tail thumped the snow underneath him without sound.

We stopped for lunch near something that looked like it

---

8) crest the top of the hill. 산꼭대기에 오르다.

could be a lake in its other life, or maybe just a womb-shaped meadow. I made peanut butter and honey sandwiches for all of us, and we opened the apricots.

"It's fabulous here." I told the dogs. "But so far it's not working."

There had never been anything wrong with my life that a few good days in the wilderness wouldn't cure, but there I sat in the middle of all those crystal-coated trees, all that diamond-studded sunshine, and I didn't feel any better. Apparently clinical depression was not like having a bad day, it wasn't even like having a lot of bad days, it was more like a house of mirrors, it was like being in a room full of one-way glass.[9]

"Come on, Mom." Jackson said. "Ski harder, go faster, climb higher."

Hailey turned her belly to the sun and groaned. "He's right." I told her. "It's all we can do."

After lunch the sun had moved behind our backs, throw in a whole different light on the path ahead of us. The snow we moved through stopped being simply white and became translucent, hinting at other colors, reflections of blues and purples and grays.

"Put your mind where your skis are." Jackson said, and we made considerably better time after that.

---

9) one way glass: a mirror that allows a person standing behind it to see through it. 관찰자만 볼 수 있고 대상이 되는 자는 볼 수 없는 거울. 예: 수사실 거울.

The sun was getting quite low in the sky when I asked Jackson if he thought we should stop to build the snow cave, and he said he'd look for the next good bank. About one hundred yards down the trail we found it, a gentle slope with eastern exposure that didn't look like it would cave in under any circumstances.[10] Jackson started to dig first.

Let me make one thing clear. I knew only slightly more about building snow caves than Jackson, having never built one, and all my knowledge coming from disaster tales of winter camping fatalities. I knew several things not to do when building a snow cave, but I was having a hard time knowing what exactly to do. But Jackson helped, and Hailey supervised, and before too long we had a little cave built, just big enough for three. We ate dinner quite pleased with our accomplishments and set the bivvy sack up inside the cave just as the sun slipped away and dusk came over Beaver Creek.

III

The temperature, which hadn't exactly soared during the day, dropped twenty degrees in as many minutes, and suddenly

---

10) a gentle slope with eastern exposure that didn't look like it would cave in under any circumstances. 동쪽으로 열려있는 완만한 경사지 (동쪽 면으로 파고 들어가 얼음집을 만들 구상임). 그 경사지는 결코 아래로 무너져 내리지(cave in) 않을 것 같이 견실함.

it didn't seem like such a great idea to change my long underwear. The original plan was to sleep with the dogs inside the bivvy sack but outside the sleeping bag, which was okay with Jackson the super-metabolizer, but not so with Hailey, the couch potato. She whined and wriggled and managed to stuff her entire fat body down inside my mummy bag, and Jackson stretched out full-length on top.

One of the unfortunate things about winter camping is that it has to happen when the days are so short. Fourteen hours is a long time to lie in a snow cave under the most perfect of circumstances. And when it's thirty-two below, or forty, fourteen hours seems like weeks.

I wish 1 could tell you I dropped right off to sleep. In truth, fear crept into my spine with the cold and I never closed my eyes. Cuddled there, amid my dogs and water bottles, I spent half of the night chastising myself for thinking I was Wonder Woman, not only risking my own life but the lives of my dogs, and other half trying to keep the numbness in my feet from crawling up to my knees.[11] When I did doze off, I'd come back to my senses

---

11) Cuddled there, amid my dogs and water bottles, I spent half of the night chastising myself for thinking I was Wonder Woman, not only risking my own life but the lives of my dogs, and other half trying to keep the numbness in my feet from crawling up to my knees. 거기에 웅크리고 누워서, 개들과 물병 사이에, 밤의 반을 나는 스스로를 자책하며 보냈다. 나를 원더우먼으로 생각한데 대하여. 분사 구문 계속됨 내 생명뿐만 아니라 개의 생명도 위험에 빠뜨리면서. 그리고 밤의 반을 발에 생긴 무감각함이 무릎 위로까지 올라오지 못하도록 애를 쓰며 보냈다.

wondering if I had frozen to death, but the alternating pain and numbness that started in my extremities and worked its way into my bones convinced me I must still be alive.12)

It was a clear night, and every now and again I would poke my head out of its nest of down and nylon13) to watch the progress of the moon across the sky. There is no doubt that it was longest and most uncomfortable night of my life.

But then the sky began to get gray, and then it began to get pink, and before too long the sun was on my bivvy sack, not warm, exactly, but holding the promise of warmth later in the day. And I ate apricots and drank Kool-Aid-flavored coffee and celebrated the rebirth of my fingers and toes, and the survival of many more important parts of my body. I sang "Rocky Mountain High" and "If I Had a Hammer." and yodeled and whistled, and even danced the two-stop14) with Jackson and let him lick my face. And when Hailey finally emerged from the sleeping bag a full hour after I did,15) we shared a peanut butter and honey sandwich and she said nothing ever tasted so

---

12) the alternating pain and numbness(추위로 아팠다 다시 무감각해졌다가 반복) that started in my extremities(몸의 제일 말단 부분. 이를테면 손가락 발가락) and worked its way into my bones convinced me I must still be alive. 손발가락부터 시작하여 뼈까지 옮겨가는 pain/numbness의 반복 때문에 아직도 살아있다는 것을 확신.

13) I would poke my head out of its nest of down and nylon 나일론과 오리털(즉 슬리핑백)으로 부터 머리를 쑥 내밀곤 했다. its nest는 슬리핑백을 nest로 비유. its의 it은 my head.

14) two-stop 춤의 한 종류.

15) a full hour after I did. 내가 슬리핑백 밖으로 나온 뒤 한 시간 뒤에야. did는 앞의 emerged from the sleeping bag을 받는 대동사. full hour는 꼭 채운 한 시간.

good. We broke camp and packed up and kicked in the snow cave with something resembling glee.[16)]

I was five miles down the trail before I realized what had happened.[17)] Not once in that fourteen-hour night did I think about deadlines, or bills, or the man in the desert.[18)] For the first time in many months I was happy to see a day beginning. The morning sunshine was like a present from the gods. What really happened, of course, is that I remembered about joy.

I know that one night out at thirty-two below doesn't sound like much to those of you who have climbed Everest or run the Iditarod or kayaked to Antarctica, and I won't try to convince you that my life was like the movies where depression goes away in one weekend, and all of life's problems vanish with a moment's clear sight.[19)] The simple truth of the matter is this:

---

16) We broke camp and packed up and kicked in the snow cave with something resembling glee. 우리는 캠프를 해체하고 짐을 꾸린 후 snow cave를 발로 차서 무너뜨렸다 (kick in). glee 비슷한 감정을 가지고. glee는 너무 기뻐 정신이 들뜬 상태.

17) I was five miles down the trail before I realized what had happened. 5 마일 정도 산을 내려와서야 나는 그동안 무슨 일이 일어났는지 깨달았다.

18) Not once in that fourteen-hour night did I think about ~ 지난 밤 14 시간 동안 단 한 번도 about 이하에 대한 생각이 들지 않았다. 부정 어귀가 문장 앞에 있어서 did I think 도치

19) I know that one night out at thirty-two below doesn't sound like much to those of you who have climbed Everest or run the Iditarod or kayaked to Antarctica, and I won't try to convince you that my life was like the movies where depression goes away in one weekend, and all of life's problems vanish with a moment's clear sight. 영하 32도인 날씨에 하룻밤 캠핑한 것은 who 이하의 경험을 한 독자 여러분(이 글은 신문 혹은 정기 간행물에 실린 글로서 독자 중 강한 아웃도어 경험자가 있을 것을 가정하고 있음 those of you. you는 독자 전반. those는 who 이하의 경험자)에게는 별 것

On Sunday I had a glimpse outside of the house of mirrors, on Saturday I couldn't have seen my way out of a paper bag.[20] And while I was skiing back toward the truck that morning, a wind came up behind us and swirled the snow around our bodies like a blizzard under blue sky. And I was struck by the simple perfection of the snowflakes, and startled by the hopefulness of sun on frozen trees.

아닌 것으로 들리겠지요.

[20] On Sunday I had a glimpse outside of the house of mirrors, on Saturday I couldn't have seen my way out of a paper bag. 이 부분은 시간의 순서대로 Saturday 이하 부분부터 읽고 그 다음 Sunday 부분을 읽어볼 것.

Comprehension Check-Up Questions

1. When and where does the story take place?

2. What makes the narrator depressed?

3. What does "clinically depressed" mean?

4. What does the doctor offer for the depression?

5. Why does the narrator love the natural world?

6. What does "my machine" mean?

7. How cold was it when the narrator spent one night on Beaver Creek?

8. How does Alex respond to the narrator when she says she is going to winter camping?

9. List the characters of Jackson and Haily.

10. xplain the visual and auditory characteristics of high mountains this morning.

11. When do the company arrive on the top of the hill and what do they do there?

12. What does the depression feel like according to the narrator?

13. Does the narrator feel better at this time?

14. Where do they build their snow cave?

15. Is the narrator good at building a snow cave?

16. When do they finish building the snow cave?

17. How cold is the night?

18. What else makes winter camping painful besides coldness?

19. Explain how painful time the narrator spent that night.

An Indian Story

Roger Jack

Roger Jack's "An Indian Story" talks about Jack, a Native American boy, who left his father house to live with his Aunt Greata. Jack's mother passed away when he was a kid and his father decides to remarry a half Native American woman who already had a child. The reason that he leaves is because he did not get along with this boy. Jack one day decided that he wants to live with his Aunt Greta. During the time that he stayed with his aunt they go on many pow-wows and traveled together learning more about the Native American beliefs. During the time that the two spent together they became really close.

(adapted from http://laker0020.blogspot.com/2004/10/indian-story.html)

Words and Phrases

heavyset, dark-complexioned, and very knowledgeable	the imitation Stonehenge Monument
big, baggy shirts	the huge outlines of the
ritual gatherings	massive hewn stones
	towered well over our heads

hair braided and clasped

accountant

agency

reservation

get into trouble

high-school dropout

legacy

transition

horse riding

dirt roads

complement

run for tribal council

tribal politics

a quarter mile

went on vacations together

trailblazers: scouts, leaders

a girlfriend of one of the guys

calling me names

the tribe's makeshift jail

bail

is always tuned in to his son

ancestors

in awe of their magnificence

Stars grew brighter

see the power of Aunt Greta

protruding through her eyes

teepee

call upon Coyote to come

and knock over these poles

drape our canvas over the

skeleton

flip out: make sb crazy

rib: ridicule

be doomed to extinction

father's footsteps

our annual treks after that

pow-wow

some local Indians I had met

performance

promissory: promise

got chapped and cracked

I

Aunt Greta was always a slow person. Grandpa used to say she was like an old lady out of the old days who never hurried herself for anything, no matter what. She was only forty-five, heavyset, dark-complexioned, and very knowledgeable of the old ways, which made her seem even older. Most of the time she wore her hair straight up or in a ponytail that hung below her beltline. At home she wore pants and big, baggy shirts, but at ritual gatherings she wore her light blue calico dress, beaded moccasins, hair braided and clasped with beaded barrettes. Sometimes she wore a scarf on her head like ladies older than she. She said we followed those we love and care for. I liked seeing her dressed for ceremonials. Even more, I liked seeing her stand before crowds of tribal members and guests translating the old language to the new for our elders, or speaking for the younger people who had no understanding of the Indian language. It made me proud to be her nephew and her son.[1]

My mom died when I was little. Dad took care of me as best as he could after that. He worked hard and earned good money as an accountant at the agency.[2] But about[3] a year after Mom died he married a half-breed Indian and this made me feel very uncomfortable. Besides, she had a child of her own who was white. We fought a lot __ me and Jeffry Pine __ and then I'd get into trouble. I was older and was supposed to know better than to misbehave.

I ran away from home one day when everyone was gone __ actually, I walked to Aunt Greta's and asked if I could move in

---

1) her nephew and her son 이모의 조카이면서 또한 아들 이모의 집에서 아들처럼 돌봄을 받으며 살아가는 필자 자신.
2) the agency 대행업체. 여기서는 인디언 보호구역에서 그 지역을 관리해주는 중앙정부 행정 대행 기관을 뜻함. 글 전체에서 사용되는 the agency는 모두 이 기관을 가리킴.
3) about: around 약.

with her. Then after I had gone to bed that night, Dad came looking for me and Aunt Greta told him what I had told her about my wanting to move in with her. He said it would be all right for a while, then we would decide what to do about it later. That[4] was a long time ago. Now I am out of high school and going to college. Meanwhile, Jeffrey Pine is a high-school dropout and living with the folks.[5]

II

Aunt Greta was married a long time ago. She married a guy named Mathew who made her very happy. They never had children, but when people asked them what was wrong, they would simply reply they were working on it. Then Mathew died during their fifth year of marriage. No children. No legacy. After that Aunt Greta took care of Grandpa. Grandpa had earlier moved in with them when Grandma died. Grandpa wasn't too old, but sometimes he acted like it. I guess it came from that long, drawn-out transition from horse riding and living out in the wild country to reservation life in dirt roads and cars.[6] He walked slowly everywhere he went; he and Aunt

---

4) that 이모 집에서 당분간 살아가기로 결정한 것.

5) folks 사람들, 여기서는 가족, 즉 dad, step-mom.

6) 말을 타고 초원(wild country: 개발하지 않은 자연 그대로의 땅)에서 살다가 길과 차로 이루어진

Greta complemented each other that way.

Eventually, Aunt Greta became interested in politics and said to run for tribal council, so Grandpa changed her Indian name from Little Girl Heart to Old Woman Walking. Aunt Greta didn't mind. In fact, she was proud of her new name. Little Girl Heart was her baby name, she said. When Grandpa died a couple of years later she was all alone. She decided tribal politics wasn't for her. Then she began teaching Indian culture and language classes. That's when I walked into her life like a newborn Mathew or Grandpa or the baby she never had. She had so much love and knowledge to share, which she passed on to me naturally and freely; she received wages for teaching others. But that was just a gesture,[7] she said.

My home and academic life improved a lot after I had moved in with her. Dad and his wife had a baby boy, and then a girl, but I didn't see too much of them. It was like we were strangers living a quarter mile from one another. Aunt Greta and I went on vacations together from the time I graduated from the eighth grade. We were trailblazers, she said, because our ancestors never traveled very far from the homeland.

보호구역으로 할아버지의 삶이 변경됨. 그 transition의 과정은 장기간에 걸쳐 천천히 진행됨. long, drawn-out transition. drawn-out은 매우 천천히.

[7] 월급 받는 것은 제스처에 불과하다. 즉 인디언 언어와 문화를 가르치는 대가로 얻는 수입은 얼마 안 된다.

III

The first year we went to Maryhill, Washington, which is about a ten-hour drive from our reservation home in Park City,[8] and saw the imitation Stonehenge Monument. We arrived there late in the evening because we had to stop off in every other town along the road to eat, whether or not we were hungry, because that was Aunt Greta's way and Grandma's and all the other old ladies of the tribe. You have to eat to survive, they would say. It was almost dark when we arrived at the park.[9] We saw the huge outlines of the massive hewn stones in a circular position. They towered well over our heads. We stood small and saw darkness fall in awe of their magnificence. Stars grew brighter and we saw them more keenly as time passed. Then they started falling, dropping out of the sky to meet us where we stood. I could see the power of Aunt Greta protruding through her eyes. She said nothing for a long time. Then, she murmured something like, "I have no teepee. I need no cover. This moment has been waiting for me here all this time." She paused. Then, "I wasn't sure what I would find here, but I'm glad we came. I was going to say something goofy like 'We should have brought the teepee and we could call upon Coyote to come and knock

---

8) Park City에 있는 우리 보호구역에서 약(about) 10시간 차로 가는 거리에 있는 Maryhill.
9) The park: Stonehenge monument 복제품이 있는 공원.

over these poles so we could drape our canvas over the skeleton and camp!' But I won't. I'm just glad we came here."

"Oh no, you aren't flipping out on me, are you?" I ribbed her. She always said good Indians remember two things: their humor and their history. These are the elements that maintain our culture and our survival in this crazy world. If these are somehow destroyed or forgotten, we would be doomed to extinction. Our power gone. And she had the biggest, silliest grin on her face. She said, "I want to camp right here!" and I knew she was serious.

We camped in the car, in the parking lot, that night. But neither of us slept until nearly daybreak. She told me Coyote stories and Indian stories and asked me what I planned to do with my life. "I want to be like you." I told her. Then she reminded me that I had a Dad to think about, too, and that maybe I should think about taking up his trade. I thought about it a lot of stories I had heard about boys following in their father's footsteps __ good or bad __ and I told Aunt Greta that I wasn't sure about living on the reservation and working at the agency all my life. Then I tried to sleep, keeping in mind everything we had talked about. I was young, but my Indian memory was good and strong.

Our annual treks after that brought us to the Olympic Penninsula on the coast and the Redwood Forest in northern

California; Yellowstone National Park in Wyoming and Glacier Park in Montana; and the Crazy Horse/ Mount Rushmore Monuments in South Dakota. We were careful in coordinating our trips with pow-wows, too. Then we talked about going all the way to Washington, D.C., and New York City to see the sights and how the other half lived, but we never did.

IV

After high-school graduation we went to Calgary for a pow-wow and I got into trouble for drinking and fighting with some local Indians I had met. The fight occurred when a girlfriend of one of the guys started acting very friendly toward me. Her boyfriend got jealous and started pushing me around and calling me names; only after I defended myself did the others join in the fight.[10] Three of us were thrown into the tribe's makeshift jail. Aunt Greta was not happy when she came to pay my bail. As a matter of fact, I had never seen her angry before. Our neighbors at the campground thought it was funny that I had been arrested and thrown into jail. I sat in the car imagining my own untimely death.[11] I was so sick.

---

10) 나 자신을 방어했을 때 다른 인디언들(즉 싸움을 걸어온 인디언의 친구들)도 싸움에 끼어들기 시작했다. 상대방이 싸움에서 밀리자 상대방의 친구들도 싸움에 합세함.

11) 이모가 하도 화가 나서 죽을 것만 같았다. untimely death는 아직 젊은 나이임에도 불구하고

I watched Aunt Greta take down the rest of the teepee with the same meticulousness with which we had set it up. I stood looking over the crowd. Lots of people had come from throughout Canada and the northern states for the pow-wow. Hundreds of people sat watching the war dance. Other people watched the stick-games and card games. But what caught my attention were the obvious drunks in the crowd. I was "one of them" now. Aunt Greta didn't talk much while we drove home. It was a long, lonely drive. We stopped only twice to eat cold, tasteless meals.

Aunt Greta didn't talk much while we drive home. When we finally got home Aunt Greta said, "Good night." and went to bed. It was only eight o'clock in the evening. I felt a heavy feeling to go talk to Dad about what had happened. So I did.

V

He was alone when I arrived at his house. As usual I walked through the front door without knocking. But he immediately called out, "Son?"

"Yeah." I said as I went to sit on a couch facing him. "How did you know it was me?"

He smiled, said hello, and told me a father is always tuned in

---

죽을 것 같은 뜻 내포

to his son. Then he sensed my hesitation to speak and asked, "What's wrong?"

"I got drunk in Calgary." My voice cracked. "I got into a fight and thrown in jail, too. Aunt Greta had to bail me out. Now she's mad at me. She hasn't said much since we packed to come home."[12]

"Did you tell her you were sorry for screwing up?" Dad asked.

"Yeah. I tried to tell her. But she clammed up on me."

"I wouldn't worry about it." Dad said. "This happens sooner or later. You really feel guilty when you take that first drink and get caught doing it.[13] Hell, when I got drunk the first time, my Mom and Dad took turns preaching to me about the evils of drinking. It didn't stop me, though, I was one of those smart asses who had to have his own way. What you have to do is come up with some sort of reparation.[14] Something that will get you back on Greta's good side."[15]

"I guess that's the problem. She didn't shout or preach to me." My voice strengthened, "But she wouldn't say anything."

"Well, Son. You have to try imagine what's going through her mind too. As much as I love you, you have been Greta's boy since you were knee-high to a grasshopper. She has tried to

---

12) 짐을 챙겨 집으로 돌아올 때 까지 말을 안했다.

13) 처음으로 술에 취하고 다른 사람이 그것을 보게 되면 guilty하게 느끼는 법이다.

14) 이제 너가 해야 할 일은 어떤 종류의 보상을 하는 것이다. 즉 술 마신 것은 할 수 없는 일이고, 단지 그 행위를 만회하는 방법을 생각해 보아라.

15) 이모를 다시 너의 좋은 쪽으로 돌리는 방법 말이다. reparation의 구체적 내용을 알려주는 부분임.

provide all the love and proper caring for you. Maybe she thinks she has done something wrong in your upbringing. She probably feels more guilty about what happened than you. Maybe she hasn't said anything because she isn't handling this very well either." Dad became less serious and said. "Of course, Greta's been drunk herself."

Stunned, I asked, "What do you mean?"

"Son, although Greta's life has changed, there are some of us who remember her younger days. She liked drinking, partying, and loud music along with dancing, stick-games, and pow-wows. She got along wherever she went looking for a good time. Another good thing about Greta was that when she found her mate and decided to settle down, she did it right.16) After she married Mathew she quit running around."

Dad smiled, "Of course, Mathew may have had some influence on her behavior, since he worked for the alcohol program."

"I wonder why she never remarried?" I asked.

"Some women just don't." Dad said. "But she had men to take care of. She had your Grandpa __ and YOU!" We laughed. Then he continued, "Greta could have had her pick of any man on the reservation.17) A lot of men chased after her before she married, and a lot of them chased after her after Mathew died. But she

---

16) 결혼을 해서 정착했을 때는 [그 이전 생활 방식을 다 버리고] 그 정착 생활을 올바르게 잘 했다.
17) 보호구역에 사는 어떤 남자라도 [짝으로] 골랐을 것이다. 가정법에 유의.

never had time for them."

"I wonder if she would have gotten married again if I hadn't moved in on her?"

"That's a question only Greta can answer. You know she may work in tribal programs and college programs, but if she had to give it all up for one reason in the world, it would be you." Dad became intent, "You are her bloodline. Otherwise I wouldn't have let you stay with her all these years.[18] The way her family believes is that two sisters coming from the same mother and father are the same. After your mother died and you asked to go and live with your Aunt, that was all right. As a matter of fact, according to her way, we were supposed to have gotten married after our period of mourning was over."

"You __ married to Aunt Greta!" I half-bellowed and again we laughed.

"Yeah. We could have made a hell of a family, don't you think?"[19] Dad tried steadying his mood. "But, you know, maybe Greta's afraid of losing you too. Maybe she's afraid that you're entering manhood and that you'll be leaving her. Like when you go away to college. You are still going to college, aren't you?"

"Yeah. But I never thought of it as leaving her. I thought it more like going out and doing what's expected of me. Ain't I

---

18) 그레타는 너의 혈육이다. 만약 혈육이 아니었으면 너를 맡기지도 않았을 것이다.

19) 그레타와 내가 결혼을 했으면 엉망진창 가족이 되었겠지? 가정법에 유의.

supposed to strike out on my own one day?"[20]

"Yeah. Your leaving your family and friends behind may be expected, but like I said, 'you are everything to Greta,' and maybe she has other plans for you." Dad looked down to the floor and I caught a glimpse of graying streaks of hair on top of his head. Then he asked me which college I planned on attending.

"One in Spokane." I answered. "I ain't decided which one yet."

VI

Then we talked about other things and a little while later his wife and the kids came home. Junior was nine, Anna Lee eight; they had gone to the last day of the tribe's celebration and carnival in Nespelem. The kids got louder as they told Dad about their carnival rides and games and prizes they had won. They shared their goodies with him. Dad looked to be having a good time eating popcorn and cotton candy.

I remembered a time when Mom and Dad brought me to the carnival. Grandpa and Grandma were with us. Mom and Dad stuck me on a big, black merry-go-round horse with flaming red nostrils and fiery eyes. Its long, dangling tongue hung out of its

---

20) 언젠가는 나의 길을 가야 하는 것 아닌가요? Be supposed to 혹은 be expected to는 주위 사람이 나에게 to 이하 하라고 기대하는 것을 뜻함.

mouth. I didn't really want to ride that horse, but I felt I had to because Grandpa kept telling Mom and Dad that I belonged on a real horse and not some wooden thing.[21] I didn't like the horse, when it hit certain angles it jolted and scared me even more. Mom and Dad offered me another ride on it, but I refused.

"Want some cotton candy?" Junior brought me back to reality. "We had fun going on the rides and trying to win some prizes. Here, you can have this one." He handed me one of his prizes. And, "Are you gonna stay with us tonight?"

I didn't realize it was after eleven o'clock.

"You can sleep in my bed." Junior offered.

"Yeah. Maybe I will, Little Brother." I said. Junior smiled. I bade everyone good night and went to his room and pulled back his top blanket revealing his Star Wars sheets.[22] I chuckled at the sight of them before lying down and trying to sleep on them. This would be my first time sleeping away from Aunt Greta in a long time. I still felt tired from my drinking and the long drive home, but I was glad to have talked to Dad. I smiled in thinking that he said he loved me, because Indian men hardly ever verbalize their emotions. I went to sleep thinking how alone Aunt Greta must have felt after I had left home and promised myself to return there as early as I could.

---

21) 내가 나무 말(즉 merry-go-around horse)이 아니라 진짜 말 후손이라고 할아버지가 자꾸 엄마 아빠에게 말하는 바람에 나는 싫어도 말을 계속 타고 있어야 할 것 같이 느껴졌다. had to [ride that horse]

22) 침대 위에 덮인 담요를 걷었다. 그랬더니 그 아래로 스타워즈 그림이 나타남.

I ate breakfast with the family before leaving. Dad told me one last thing that he and Aunt Greta had talked about sometime before. "You know, she talked about giving you an Indian name. She asked me if you had one and I said 'no,' She talked about it and I thought maybe she would go ahead and do it too but her way of doing this is: boys are named for their father's side and girls are named for their mother's. Maybe she's still waiting for me to give you a name. I don't know."

"I remember when Grandpa named her, but I never thought of having a name myself. What was the name?" I asked.

"I don't remember. Something about stars."

VII

Aunt Greta was sitting at the kitchen table drinking coffee and listening to an Elvis album when I got home. Elvis always made her lonesome for the old days or it cheered her up when she felt down. I didn't know what to say, but showed her the toy totem pole Junior had given me.

"That's cute." she said. "So you spent the night at the carnival?"

"No. Junior gave it to me." I explained. "I camped at Dad's"

"Are you hungry?" she was about to get up from the table.

"No. I've eaten." I saw a stack of pancakes on the stove.

I hesitated another moment before asking. "What's with Elvis?"

"He's dead!" she said and smiled, because that's what I usually said to her. "Oh well, I just needed a little cheering up, I guess."

I remember hearing a story about Aunt Greta that happened a long time ago. She was a teenager when the Elvis craze hit the reservation.[23] Back then hardly any families had television sets, so they couldn't see Elvis. But when his songs hit the airwaves on the radio, the girls went crazy. Elvis had a concert in Seattle and my Mom and Aunt Greta and a couple other girls went to it. Legend said that Elvis kissed Aunt Greta on the cheek during his performance and she took to heart the old "ain't never going to wash that cheek again" promissory and never washed her cheek for a long time and it got chapped and cracked until Grandpa and Grandma finally had to order her to go to the clinic to get some medicine to clean up her face. She hated them for a while, still swearing Elvis would be her number one man forever.

"How's your Dad?"

"He' all right. The kids were at the carnival when I got to his house, so we had a nice, long visit." I paused momentarily before adding, "And he told me some stories about you too."

"Oh?"

"Yeah. He said you were quite a fox when you were young. And

23) Elvis craze/ hit/ the reservation.

he said you probably could have had any man you wanted before you married Uncle Mathew, and you could have had any man after Uncle Mathew died. So, did you never find another husband?"

Aunt Greta sat quietly for a moment. "It's just that after my Mathew died I didn't want anyone else. He was so good to me that I didn't think I could find any better. Besides, I had you and Grandpa to care for, didn't I? Have I ever complained about that?"

I persisted, "But haven't you ever thought about what might have happened if you had gotten married again? You might have done like Dad and started a whole new family. Babies, even!"

Aunt Greta was truly embarrassed. "Will you get away from here with talk like that? I don't need babies. Probably very soon you'll be bringing them home for me to take care of anyhow."

We got along great after that conversation.24) It was like we had never gone to Calgary and I had never gotten on to her wrong side at all. We were like kids rediscovering what it was worth to have a real good friend go away for a while and then come back. To be appreciative of each other, I imagined Aunt Greta might have said.

---

24) 그 대화 후 우리는 다시 사이가 좋아졌다. get along 사이좋게 지내다.

VIII

Our trip to Calgary happened in July. August and September found me dumbfounded as to what to do with myself college-wise. I felt grateful that Indian parents don't throw out their offspring when they reach a certain age. Aunt Greta said it was too late for fall term and that I should rest my brain for a while and think about going to college after Christmas. So I explored different schools in the area and talked to people who had gone to them. Meanwhile, some of my friends were going to Haskell Indian Junior College in Kansas. Aunt Greta frowned upon my going there. She said it was too far away from home, people die of malaria there, and if you're not drunk, you're just crazy. So I stuck with the Spokane plan.

That fall Aunt Greta was invited to attend a language seminar in Portland. She taught Indian language classes when asked to. So we decided to take a side trip to our old campsite at Stonehenge. This time we arrived early in the morning and it was foggy and drizzling rain. The sight of the stones didn't provide the feeling we had experienced earlier. To us, the sight seemed to be just a bunch of rocks standing, overlooking the Columbia River, a lot of sagebrush, and two highways. It didn't offer us feelings of mysticism and power anymore. Unhappy with the mood, Aunt Greta said we might leave; her words hung heavy on the air.[25]

We stayed in Portland for a week and then made it a special point to leave late in the afternoon so we could stop by Stonehenge again at dusk. So with careful planning we arrived with just enough light to take a couple pictures and then darkness began settling in.[26] We sat in the car eating baloney sandwiches and potato chips and drinking pop because we were tired of restaurant food and we didn't want people staring at us when we ate. That's where we were when an early evening star fell. Aunt Greta's mouth fell open, potato chip crumbs clung to the sides of her mouth. "This is it!" she squealed in English, Indian, and English again. "Get out of the car, Son." and she half pushed me out the door. "Go and stand in the middle of the circle and pray for something good to happen to you." I ran out and stood waiting and wondering what was supposed to happen. I knew better than to doubt Aunt Greta's wishes or superstitions. Then the moment came to pass.

"Did you feel it?" she asked as she led me back to the car.

"I don't know." I told her because I didn't think anything had happened.

"I guess it just takes some people a little longer to realize." she said.

---

25) 이모의 목소리가 공기 중에 무겁게 걸렸다. 즉 침울한 목소리로 말했다.

26) 세심하게 계획을 세워 우리는 Stonehenge에 도착했다. 사진 두 장을 찍을 만큼의 빛이 남아있을 때 도착, 그리고는 곧 어둠이 내림.

I never quite understood what was supposed to have happened that day. A couple months later I was packing up to move to Spokane. I decided to go into the accounting business, like Dad. Aunt Greta quizzed me hourly before I was to leave whether I was all right and if I would be all right in the city. "Yeah, yeah." I heard myself repeating. So by the time I really was to leave she clued me in on her new philosophy: it wasn't that I was leaving her, it was just that she wouldn't be around to take care of me much anymore. She told me, "Good Indians stick together." and that I should search out our people who were already there, but not forget those who were still at home.

After I arrived in Spokane and settle down I went home. Then my studies got to intense that I didn't think I could travel home as much anymore. So I stayed in Spokane a lot more than before. Finally I didn't worry as much about the folks at home. I would be out walking in the evening and know someone's presence was with me. I never bothered telephoning Dad at his office at the agency; and I never knew where or when Aunt Greta worked. She might have been at the agency or school. Then one day Dad telephoned me at school. After asking how I was doing, he told me why he was calling. "Your Aunt Greta is sick. The doctors don't know what's wrong with her yet. They just told me to advise her family of the possibility that it could be serious." I only half heard what he was saying, "Son, are you there?"

"Yeah."

"Did you hear me? Did you hear what I said?"

"Yeah. I don't think you have to worry about Aunt Greta, though. She'll be all right. Like the old people used to say, 'she might go away for a while, but she'll be back,'" and I hung up the telephone unalarmed.

Comprehension Check-Up Questions

1. Describe Aunt Greta. How old is she? What characteristics does she hold?

2. How come did the writer live with the aunt not with his parents?

3. How old is the writer at this time approximately?

4. Describe Mathew, Aunt Greta's deceased husband.

5. From when did the aunt start to take care of Grandpa?

6. How much did the writer's life improve after his living with the aunt?

7. Why did the writer and aunt arrive late at the imitation Stonehenge Monument?

8. Describe the Stonehenge landscape they saw together.

9. How did the aunt appear when she saw the stars falling?

10. Where did they stay that night and what did the aunt tell?

11. When did they go to Calgary pow-wow?

12. What trouble did the writer get in there and why?

13. How did the aunt feel about that incident?

14. Why did the writer go to Dad instead of staying at the aunt's?

15. According to Dad how was the aunt at her youth?

16. Why does Dad assume the aunt decide to care of the writer?

17. How old are Junior and Anna Lee?

18. Where did the writer stay that night? And how did he feel now?

19. What was the aunt doing when the writer came back home?

20. How much did the aunt love Elvis?

21. Why does the aunt say she did not get remarried after Mathew's death?

22. How does the conversation with the aunt affect the writer's feeling?

23. Why does the aunt oppose to the writer's going to a college far away from home?

24. Describe two visits to Stonehenge.

25. In what city does the writer's college locate?

26. What in college made him visit home less and less frequently?

27. What happened to the aunt according to Dad's call?

Mute in an English-Only Society

Chang-rae Lee

Chang-Rae Lee is a Korean American novelist, He was born in 1965 in Korea. He left Korea when he was three years old and emigrated in the US with his family. He was raised in New York, and graduated from Yale University of Oregon with a MFA in writing. His works are *Native Speaker* (1995), *A Gesture Life* (1999), *Aloft* (2004), and *The Surrendered* (2010). He is recipient of the Hemingway Foundation/PEN Award and Asian/Pacific American Awards for Literature amongst others, and a nominated finalist for the 2011 Pulitzer Prize for Fiction.

Words and Phrases

proliferation	sundry
main commercial strip	readied speech
longtime residents	harrowing
alienated and even unwelcome	venture
exclusionary ideas	ocean liner
exacting	bounty

descendants	spot vt.
Italian pastry	resolved
Jewish tailors and cleaners	nudged
hold off	glass display
dotting	unnerved
loathed	double-parked
playing catch	shooing
nasality	flooded the engine
ham and mimic	sedan
crack up	glove compartment
pock workbook	brittle and dog-eared
stick-figure	fashion vt.
compound sentences	plain paper wrapping

When I read the trouble of reading in Palisades Park, New Jersey, over the proliferation of Korean-language signs along its main commercial strip, I unexpectedly sympathized with the frustrations, resentments, and fears of the longtime residents. They clearly felt alienated and even unwelcome in a vital part of their community. The town, like seven others in New Jersey, has passed laws requiring that half of any commercial sign in a foreign language be in English.

Now I certainly would never tolerate any exclusionary ideas

about who could rightfully settle and belong in the town. But having been raised in a Korean immigrant family, I saw every day the exacting price and power of language, especially with my mother, who was an outsider in an English-only world. In the first years we lived in America, my mother could speak only the most basic English, and she often encountered great difficulty whenever she went out.

We live in New Rochelle, New York, in the early seventies, and most of the local businesses were run by the descendants of immigrants who, generations ago, had come to the suburbs from New York City. Proudly dotting Main Street and North Avenue were Italian pastry and cheese shops, Jewish tailors and cleaners, and Polish and German butchers and bakers.[1] If my mother's marketing couldn't wait until the weekend, when my father had free time, she would often hold off until I came home from school to buy the groceries.[2]

Though I was only six or seven years old, she insisted that I go out shopping with her and my younger sister. I mostly loathed the task,[3] partly because it meant I couldn't spend the afternoon off playing catch with my friends but also because I knew our errands[4] would inevitably lead to an awkward scene, and that I would have

---

1) 도치 문장에 유의.
2) 어머니는 내가 하교할 때까지 식료품 사러 가기를 멈추고 있었다. would는 과거의 불규칙한 습관.
3) the task는 어머니 장보기에 함께 가는 일.
4) 어머니, 여동생과 장보는 일.

to speak up to help my mother.

I was just learning the language myself, but I was a quick study, as children are with new tongues. I had spent kindergarten in almost complete silence, hearing only the high nasality of my teacher and comprehending little but cranky wails and cries of my classmates. But soon, seemingly mere months later, I had already become a terrible ham and mimic, and I would crack up my father with impressions of teachers, his friends, and even himself. My mother scolded me for aping his speech,[5] and the one time I attempted to make light of hers I rated a roundhouse smack on my bottom.[6]

For her, the English language was not very funny. It usually meant trouble and a good dose of shame, and sometimes real hurt. Although she had a good reading knowledge of the language from university classes in South Korea, she had never practiced actual conversation. So in America she used English flash cards and phrase books and watched television with us kids. And she faithfully carried a pocket workbook illustrated with stick-figure people and compound sentences to be filled in.

But none of it seemed to do her much good. Staying mostly at home to care for us, she didn't have many chances to try out sundry words and phrases. When she did, say, at the window of

---

5) 아버지의 (영어로 하는)말을 흉내 내는 것에 대해 어머니가 뭐라 하심.
6) 어머니 영어 흉내를 냈을 때 어머니에게 엉덩이를 맞음.

the post office, her readied speech would stall, freeze, sometimes altogether collapse.

One day was unusually harrowing. We ventured downtown in the new Ford County Squire my father had bought her, an enormous station wagon that seemed as long __ and deft __ as an ocean liner. We were shopping for a special meal for guests visiting that weekend, and my mother had heard that a particular butcher carried fresh oxtails, which she needed for a traditional soup.

We'd never been inside the shop, but my mother would pause before its window, which was always lined with whole hams, crown roasts, and ropes of plump handmade sausages. She greatly esteemed the bounty with her eyes, and my sister and I did also, but despite our desirous cries she'd turn us away and instead buy the packaged links at the Finast supermarket, where she felt comfortable looking them over and could easily spot the price. And, of course, not have to talk.

But that day she was resolved. The butcher store was crowded, and as we stepped inside, the door jingled a welcome. No one seemed to notice. We waited for some time, and people who entered after us were now being served. Finally an old woman nudged my mother and waved a little ticket, which we hadn't taken. We patiently waited again, until one of the beefy men behind the glass display hollered our number.

My mother pulled us forward and began searching the cases, but the oxtails were nowhere to be found. The man, his big arms crossed,[7] sharply said, "Come on, lady, whaddya want?" This unnerved her, and she somehow blurted the Korean word for oxtail, soggori.

The butcher looked as if my mother had put something sour in his mouth, and he glanced back at the lighted board and called the next number.

Before I knew it, she had rushed us outside and back in the wagon, which she had double-parked because of the crowd. She was furious, almost vibrating with fear and grief, and I could see she was about to cry.

She wanted to go back inside, but now the driver of the car we were blocking wanted to pull out.[8] She was shooing us away. My mother, who had just earned her driver's license, started furiously working the pedals. But in her haste she must have flooded the engine, for it wouldn't turn over. The driver started honking and then another car began honking as well, and soon it seemed the entire street was shrieking at us.

In the following years, my mother grew steadily more comfortable with English. In Korean she could be fiery, stern, deeply funny, and ironic, in English just slightly less so.[9] If she

---

7) 팔짱을 낀 채.
8) 우리 차가 막고 있었던 차가 빠져나가려고 했다.
9) so는 앞의 여러 형용사(fiery, stern, deeply funny, and ironic)를 대신 받음.

was never quite fluent, she gained enough confidence to make herself clearly known to anyone, and particularly to me.

Five years ago she died of cancer, and some months after we buried her I found myself in the driveway of my father's house, washing her sedan. I liked taking care of her things; it made me feel close to her. While I was cleaning out the glove compartment, I found her pocket English workbook, the one with the silly illustrations. I hadn't seen it in neasrly twenty years. The yellowed pages were brittle and dog-eared. She had fashioned a plain paper wrapping for it, and I wondered whether she meant to protect the book or hide it.

I don't doubt that she would have appreciated doing the family shopping on the new Broad Avenue of Palisades Park. But I like to think, too, that she would have understood those who now complain about the Korean-only signs.

I wonder what these same people would have done if they had seen my mother studying her English workbook __ or lost in a store. Would they have nodded gently at her? Would they have lent a kind word?

Stories

Too Soon a Woman

Dorothy Marie Johnson

Dorothy Marie Johnson (1905–1984) was born in McGregor, Iowa, the only daughter of Lester Eugene Johnson and Mary Louisa Barlow. Soon after her birth, the family moved to Montana.

While she was a student at Whitefish High School she began to write professionally, working as a newspaper stringer for *The Daily Inter Lake* in Kalispell, Montana. She studied English in college before a brief marriage which ended with a divorce.

Her writing career seemed to take off in 1935 when she sold her first short story to *The Saturday Evening Post* for the sum of $400. But Johnson did not sell another story for 11 years until, in 1941, four stories narrated by a recurring character, "Beulah Bunny." sold to *The Saturday Evening Post* for $2,100. Her writing was temporarily sidetracked by World War II, when she went to work for the Air Warden Service. After the war, she produced some of her best-known Western stories. Three of these would later be made into notable films, *namely A Man Called Horse* (1950), *The Man Who Shot Liberty Valance* (1953) and *The Hanging Tree* (1957).

mile by slow mile	game
skimpy	venison
romped and trotted	homesteaders
conestoga	brought in
weary	porcupine
woods town	rigged up the tarp sheet
two-bit sawmill	wore out
teamsters	grades
prid'near: dialect of pretty near	deep-rutted roads
out of grub	gaunt
prairie	grim
timber claims	pardner: dialect of partner
past worrying	butcher
starvin': starving	hetts: dialect of has
plodded off	soon's as: as soon as
racket	growl
pitch dark	squalling
plumb	pine cone
clearing	pack horse
hide	sedately

I

We left the home place behind, mile by slow mile, heading for the mountains, across the prairie where the wind blew forever.

At first there were four of us with the one-horse wagon and its skimpy load. Pa and I walked, because I was a big boy of eleven. My two little sisters romped and trotted until they got tired and had to be boosted up into the wagon bed.

That was no covered Conestoga, like Pa's folks came West in, but just an old farm wagon, drawn by one weary horse, creaking and rumbling westward to the mountains, toward the little woods town where Pa thought he had an old uncle who owned a little two-bit sawmill.

Two weeks we had been moving when we picked up Mary, who had run away from somewhere that she wouldn't tell. Pa didn't want her along, but she stood up to him with no fear in her voice.

"I'd rather go with a family and look after kids." she said, "but I ain't going back. If you won't take me, I'll travel with any wagon that will."

Pa scowled at her, and her wide blue eyes stared back.

"How old are you?" he demanded.

"Eighteen." she said. "There's teamsters come this way sometimes. I'd rather go with you folks. But I won't go back."

"We're prid'near out of grub." my father told her. "We're clean out of money. I got all I can handle without taking anybody else." He turned away as if he hated the sight of her. "You'll have to walk." he said.

So she went along with us and looked after the little girls, but Pa wouldn't talk to her.

On the prairie, the wind blew. But in the mountains, there was rain. When we stopped at little timber claims along the way, the homesteaders said it had rained all summer. Crops among the blackened stumps were rotted and spoiled.[1] There was no cheer anywhere, and little hospitality. The people we talked to were past worrying. They were scared and desperate.

So was Pa. He traveled twice as far each day as the wagon, ranging through the woods with his rifle, but he never saw game. He had been depending on venison, but we never got any except as a grudging gift from the homesteaders.

He brought in a porcupine once, and that was fat meat and good. Mary roasted it in chunks over the fire, half crying with the smoke. Pa and I rigged up the tarp sheet for shelter to keep the rain from putting the fire clean out.

The porcupine was long gone, except for some of the tried-out fat that Mary had saved, when we came to an old, empty cabin. Pa said we'd have to stop. The horse was wore

---

1) (습기로) 검게 된 나무 그루터기 사이로 작물들이 썩고 망가져 있었다.

out, couldn't pull anymore up those grades on the deep-rutted roads in the mountains.

At the cabin, at least there was shelter. We had a few potatoes left and some cornmeal. There was a creek that probably had fish in it, if a person could catch them. Pa tried it for half a day before he gave up. To this day I don't care for fishing. I remember my father's sunken eyes in his gaunt, grim face.

He took Mary and me outside the cabin to talk. Rain dripped on us from branches overhead.

"I think I know where we are." he said. "I calculate to get to old John's and back in about four days.[2] There'll be grub in the town, and they'll let me have some whether old John's still there or not."

He looked at me. "You do like she tells you."[3] he warned. It was the first time he had admitted Mary was on earth since we picked her up two weeks before.

"You're my pardner." he said to me, "but it might be she's got more brains. You mind what she says."

He burst out with bitterness, "There ain't anything good left in the world, or people to care if you live or die. But I'll get grub in the town and come back with it."

He took a deep breath and added, "If you get too all-fired

2) 존 집에 갔다가 사흘 후 돌아오겠다. calculate는 일정을 계산해 보니 그렇게 하면 되겠다의 의미.
3) 메리가 하라는 대로 해라. like=as.

hungry, butcher the horse. It'll be better than starvin'."

He kissed the little girls goodbye and plodded off through the woods with one blanket and the rifle.

II

The cabin was moldy and had no floor. We kept a fire going under a hole in the roof, so it was full of blinding smoke, but we had to keep the fire so as to dry out the wood.

The third night we lost the horse. A bear scared him. We heard the racket, and Mary and I ran out, but we couldn't see anything in the pitch dark.

In gray daylight I went looking for him, and I must have walked fifteen miles. It seemed like I had to have that horse at the cabin when Pa came or he'd whip me. I got plumb lost two or three times and thought maybe I was going to die there alone and nobody would ever know it, but I found the way back to the clearing.

That was the fourth day, and Pa didn't come. That was the day we ate up the last of the grub.

The fifth day, Mary went looking for the horse. My sisters whimpered, huddled in a quilt by the fire, because they were scared and hungry.

I never did get dried out, always having to bring in more damp wood and going out to yell to see if Mary would hear me and not get lost. But I couldn't cry like the little girls did, because I was a big boy, eleven years old.

It was near dark when there was an answer to my yelling, and Mary came into the clearing.

Mary didn't have the horse — we never saw hide nor hair of that old horse again — but she was carrying something big and white that looked like a pumpkin with no color to it.

She didn't say anything, just looked around and saw Pa wasn't there yet, at the end of the fifth day.

"What's that thing?" my sister Elizabeth demanded.

"Mushroom." Mary answered. "I bet it hefts ten pounds."

"What are you going to do with it now?" I sneered. "Play football here?"

"Eat it — maybe." she said, putting it in a corner. Her wet hair hung over her shoulders. She huddled by the fire.

My sister Sarah began to whimper again. "I'm hungry!" she kept saying.

"Mushrooms ain't good eating." I said. "They can kill you."

"Maybe." Mary answered. "Maybe they can. I don't set up to know all about everything, like some people."

"What's that mark on your shoulder?" I asked her. "You tore your dress on the brush."

"What do you think it is?" she said, her head bowed in the smoke.

"Looks like scars." I guessed.

"'This scars. They whipped me. Now mind your own business. I want to think."

Elizabeth whimpered, "Why don't Pa come back?"

"He's coming." Mary promised. "Can't come in the dark. Your pa'll take care of you soon's he can."

She got up and rummaged around in the grub box.

"Nothing there but empty dishes." I growled. "If there was anything, we'd know it."

Mary stood up. She was holding the can with the porcupine grease.

"I'm going to have something to eat." she said coolly. "You kids can't have any yet. And I don't want any squalling, mind."

It was a cruel thing, what she did then. She sliced that big, solid mushroom and heated grease in a pan.

The smell of it brought the little girls out of their quilt, but she told them to go back in so fierce a voice that they obeyed.[4]

They cried to break your heart.

I didn't cry. I watched, hating her.

I endured the smell of the mushroom frying as long as I

---

4) 버섯 향으로 동생들이 이불 밖으로 나왔다. 그러나 메리는 단호한 목소리도 다시 이불 속으로 들어가라고 해서 동생들이 다시 들어갔다. so that 용법.

could. Then I said, "Give me some."

"Tomorrow." Mary answered. "Tomorrow, maybe. But not tonight." She turned to me with a sharp command: "Don't bother me! Just leave me be."

She knelt there by the fire and finished frying the slice of mushroom.

If I'd had Pa's rifle, I'd have been willing to kill her right then and there.

She didn't eat right away. She looked at the brown, fried slice for a while and said, "By tomorrow morning, I guess you can tell whether you want any."

The little girls stared at her as she ate. Sarah was chewing an old leather glove.

When Mary crawled into the quilts with them, they moved away as far as they could get.

I was so scared that my stomach heaved, empty as it was.[5]

Mary didn't stay in the quilts long. She took a drink out of the water bucket and sat down by the fire and looked through the smoke at me.

She said in a low voice, "I don't know how it will be if it's poison. Just do the best you can with the girls. Because your pa will come back, you know.... You better go to bed. I'm going to sit up."

---

5) empty as it was: although it was empty.

And so would you sit up. If it might be your last night on earth and the pain of death might seize you at any moment, you would sit up by the smoky fire, wide awake, remembering whatever you had to remember, savoring life.

We sat in silence after the girls had gone to sleep. Once I asked, "How long does it take?"

"I never heard." she answered. "Don't think about it."

I slept after a while, with my chin on my chest. Maybe Peter dozed that way at Gethsemane as the Lord knelt praying.

III

Mary's moving around brought me wide awake. The black of night was fading.

"I guess it's all right." Mary said. "I'd be able to tell by now, wouldn't I?"

I answered gruffly, "I don't know."

Mary stood in the doorway for a while, looking out at the dripping world as if she found it beautiful. Then she fried slices of the mushroom while the little girls danced with anxiety.

We feasted, we three, my sisters and I, until Mary ruled, "That'll hold you." and would not cook any more. She didn't touch any of the mushroom herself.

That was a strange day in the moldy cabin. Mary laughed and was gay; she told stories, and we played "Who's Got the Thimble?" with a pine cone.

In the afternoon we heard a shout, and my sisters screamed and I ran ahead of them across the clearing.

The rain had stopped. My father came plunging out of the woods leading a pack horse __ and well I remember the treasures of food in that pack.

He glanced at us anxiously as he tore at the ropes that bound the pack.

"Where's the other one?" he demanded.

Mary came out of the cabin then, walking sedately. As she came toward us, the sun began to shine.

My stepmother was a wonderful woman.

Comprehension Check-Up Questions

1. Where are the narrator's family headed?

2. How do the family meet Mary on the way and why does she go along with them?

3. Why doesn't the father want Mary to accompany them at first?

4. What troubles do they confront at the cabin?

5. How does the narrator react to the loss of the horse?

6. Why doesn't Mary allow the children to eat mushrooms?

7. What role does Mary eventually have in the family?

8. Think about the title of the story and explain why it is a good one?

A Day's Wait

Ernest Hemingway

Ernest Miller Hemingway (1899–1961) was an American journalist, novelist, short-story writer, and sportsman. His economical and understated style — which he termed the iceberg theory — had a strong influence on 20th-century fiction, while his adventurous lifestyle and his public image brought him admiration from later generations. Hemingway produced most of his work between the mid-1920s and the mid-1950s, and he won the Nobel Prize in Literature in 1954. He published seven novels, six short-story collections, and two non-fiction works. Three of his novels, four short-story collections, and three non-fiction works were published posthumously. Many of his works are considered classics of American literature.

Words and Phrases	
ache	slither
purgative	flush
acid	covey
germ	mound

pneumonia [nju:'mounjə]	be poised
bother	flush
light-headed	hold tight on o.s.
sleet [sli:t]	thermometer
varnish	relax
setter	slack
slip	

I

He came into the room to shut the windows while we were still in bed and I saw he looked ill. He was shivering, his face was white, and he walked slowly as though it ached to move. "What's the matter, Schatz?"

"I've got a headache."

"You better go back to bed."

"No. I'm all right."

"You go to bed. I'll see you when I'm dressed."

But when I came downstairs he was dressed, sitting by the fire, looking a very sick and miserable boy of nine years. When I put my hand on his forehead I knew he had a fever.

"You go up to bed." I said, "you're sick."

"I'm all right." he said.

When the doctor came he took the boy's temperature.

"What is it?" I asked him.

"One hundred and two."

Downstairs, the doctor left three different medicines in different colored capsules with instructions for giving them. One was to bring down the fever, another a purgative, the third to overcome an acid condition. The germs of influenza can only exist in an acid condition, he explained. He seemed to know all about influenza and said there was nothing to worry about if the fever did not go above one hundred and four degrees. This was a light epidemic of flu and there was no danger if you avoided pneumonia.

Back in the room I wrote the boy's temperature down and made a note of the time to give the various capsules.

"Do you want me to read to you?"

"All right. If you want to." said the boy. His face was very white and there were dark areas under his eyes. He lay still in the bed and seemed very detached from what was going on. I read aloud from Howard Pyle's Book of Pirates; but I could see he was not following what I was reading.

"How do you feel, Schatz?" I asked him.

"Just the same, so far." he said.

I sat at the foot of the bed and read to myself while I waited for it to be time to give another capsule. It would have been natural for him to go to sleep, but when I looked up he was looking at the foot of the bed, looking very strangely.

"Why don't you try to go to sleep? I'll wake you up for the medicine."

"I'd rather stay awake."

After a while he said to me, "You don't have to stay in here with me, Papa, if it bothers you."

"It doesn't bother me."

"No, I mean you don't have to stay if it's going to bother you."

I thought perhaps he was a little lightheaded and after giving him the prescribed capsules at eleven o'clock I went out for a while.

II

It was a bright, cold day, the ground covered with a sleet that had frozen so that it seemed as if all the bare trees, the bushes, the cut brush and all the grass and the bare ground had been varnished with ice. I took the young Irish setter for a little walk up the road and along a frozen creek, but it was difficult to stand or walk on the glassy surface and the red dog slipped and slithered and I fell twice, hard, once dropping my gun and having it slide away over the ice.

We flushed a covey of quail under a high clay bank with overhanging brush and I killed two as they went out of sight over the top of the bank. Some of the covey lit in trees, but most of them scattered into brush piles and it was necessary to jump on the ice-coated mounds of brush several times before they would flush. Coming out while you were poised unsteadily on the icy, springy brush they made difficult shooting and I killed two, missed five, and started back pleased to have found a covey close to the house and happy there were so many left to find on another day.

At the house they said the boy had refused to let any one come into the room.

"You can't come in." he said. "You mustn't get what I have."

I went up to him and found him in exactly the position I had left him, white-faced, but with the tops of his cheeks flushed by the fever, staring still, as he had stared, at the foot of the bed.

I took his temperature.

"What is it?"

"Something like a hundred." I said. It was one hundred and two and four tenths.

"It was a hundred and two." he said.

"Who said so?"

"The doctor."

III

"Your temperature is all right." I said. "It's nothing to worry about."

"I don't worry." he said, "but I can't keep from thinking."

"Don't think." I said. "Just take it easy."

"I'm taking it easy." he said and looked straightahead. He was evidently holding tight onto himself about something.

"Take this with water."

"Do you think it will do any good?"

"Of course it will."

I sat down and opened the Pirate book and commenced to read, but I could see he was not following, so I stopped.

"About what time do you think I'm going to die?" he asked.

"What?"

"About how long will it be before I die?"

"You aren't going to die. What's the matter with you?"

"Oh, yes, I am. I heard him say a hundred and two."

"People don't die with a fever of one hundred and two. That's a silly way to talk."

"I know they do. At school in France the boys told me you can't live with forty-four degrees. I've got a hundred and two."

He had been waiting to die all day, ever since nine o'clock in the morning.

"You poor Schatz." I said. "Poor old Schatz. It's like miles and kilometres. You aren't going to die. That's a different thermometer. On that thermometer thirty-seven is normal. On this kind it's ninety-eight."

"Are you sure?"

"Absolutely." I said. "It's like miles and kilometers. You know, like how many kilometers we make when we do seventy miles in the car?"

"Oh." he said.

But his gaze at the foot of the bed relaxed slowly. The hold over himself relaxed too, finally, and the next day it was very slack and he cried very easily at little things that were of no importance.

Comprehension Check-Up Questions

1. In what season does the story take place?

2. How does the father know his son is sick?

3. Why does the father go outside leaving his son sick?

4. What does the father do outside while his son is resting in bed?

5. How much time passes from the beginning of the story until the end?

6. Why does the boy cry easily the next day?

7. What is the boy waiting for?

My Father Sits in the Dark

Jerome Weidman

Jerome Weidman (1913-1998) was an American playwright and novelist. Weidman was born in Manhattan, New York City, and moved with his family to The Bronx after finishing high school at DeWitt Clinton. His parents were Jewish immigrants and his father worked in the garment trade. He also worked in the garment industry, which later provided him with book material, and attended City College of New York and New York University Law School, all the while writing stories and finally novels.

In his work he wrote about the "rough underside of business and politics __ and daily life __ in New York." The Independent obituary states: "There was precious little hope of salvation __ indeed, precious little hope __ in his early novels and often dazzling and highly crafted short stories, many of which inevitably found their way into New Yorker during the late Thirties and early Forties."

I

My father has a peculiar habit. He is fond of sitting in the dark, alone. Sometimes I come home very late. The house is dark. I let myself in quietly because I do not want to disturb my mother. She is a light sleeper.[1] I tiptoe into the room and undress in the dark. I go to the kitchen for a drink of water. My bare feet make no noise. I step into the room and almost trip over my father. He is sitting in a kitchen chair, in his pajamas, smoking his pipe.

"Hello, Pop." I say.

---

1) light sleeper 잠을 깊이 자지 못하는 사람.

"Hello, son."

"Why don't you go to bed, Pa?"

"I will." he says.

But he remains there. Long after I am asleep I hear my mother get the house ready for the night. I hear my kid brother go to bed. I hear my sister come in.

I hear her do things with jars and combs until she, too, is quiet.[2] I know she has gone to sleep. In a little while I hear my mother say good night to my father. I continue to read. Soon I become thirsty(I drink a lot of water). I go to the kitchen for a drink. Again I almost stumble across my father. Many times it startles me. I forget about him. And there he is smoking, sitting, thinking.

"Why don't you go to bed, Pop?"

" I will, son."

But he doesn't. He just sits there and smokes and thinks. It worries me. I can't understand it. What can he be thinking about? Once I asked him.

"What are you thinking about, Pa?"

"Nothing." he said.

Once I left him there and went to bed. I awoke several hours later. I was thirsty. I went to the kitchen. There he was. His pipe was out. But he sat there, staring into a corner of the

---

2) I hear her do things with jars and combs 누나가 화장품이나 빗을 만지는 소리가 들린다. jars는 화장품병.

kitchen. After a moment I became accustomed to the darkness. I took my drink. He still sat and stared. His eyes did not blink. I thought he was not even aware of me. I was afraid.

"Why don't you go to bed, Pop?"

"I will, son." he said. Don't wait up for me."

"But." I said, "you've been sitting here for hours. What's wrong? What are you thinking about?"

"Nothing, son." he said. "Nothing. It's just restful. That's all."

The way he said it was convincing. He did not seem worried. His voice was even and pleasant. It always is. But I could not understand it. How could it be restful to sit alone in an uncomfortable chair far into the night, in darkness?

What can it be?

I review all the possibilities.[3] It can't be money. I know that. We haven't much, but when he is worried about money he makes no secret of it. It can't be his health. He is not reticent about that either. It can't be the health of anyone in the family. We are a bit short on money, but we are long on health(Knock wood, my mother would say).[4] What can it be? I am afraid I do not know. But that does not stop me from worrying.

---

3) I review all the possibilities. 모든 가능성(아버지가 밤에 불도 안 켜고 앉아계시는 이유)들을 다 헤아려본다.

4) 우리는 돈은 모자랐지만(short) 건강은 좋았다. 모자라다의 뜻을 가진 'short'에 대해 'long'을 대비시킨 pun. 괄호 속은 어머니가 이 말을 들으시면 'Knock wood'하라고 하실 것이다. 가정법. knock wood는 앞서 한 말이 부정(bad luck)으로 작용할까봐 테이블 등을 두드리는 행위.

Maybe he is thinking of his brothers in the old country. Or of his mother and two step-mothers. Or of his father. But they are all dead. And he would not brood about them like that. I say brood, but it is not really true. He does not brood. He does not seem to be thinking. He looks too peaceful, too, well not contented, just too peaceful, to be brooding. Perhaps it is as he says. Perhaps it is restful. But it does not seem possible. It worries me.

If I only knew that what he thinks about.[5] I might not be able to help him. He might not even need help. It may be as he says. It may be restful. But at least I would not worry about it.

Why does he just sit there, in there dark? Is his mind failing?[6] No, it can't be. He is only fifty-three. And he is just as keen-witted as ever. In fact, he is the same in every respect. He still likes beet soup. He still reads the second section of the Times first. He still wears wing collars.[7] He still believes that Debs[8] could have saved the country and that T.R. was a tool of the moneyed interests.[9] He is the same in every way. He does not even look older that he did five years ago. Everybody

---

5) If I only knew what he thinks about. 아버지가 뭘 생각하시는지 알기만 한다면. if only... 하기만 한다면. 그리고 가정법 시제. 뒤에 나오는 I might not be able to help him. 도 연결되면서 가정법 시제.

6) Is his mind failing? 정신이 이상한가? fail은 정상대로 작동하지 못하는 상태.

7) wing collars. 앞부분이 살짝 접힌 칼라.

8) Debs. Eugene Debs. 미국의 사회주의자.

9) T.R. was a tool of the moneyed interests. Theodore Roosevelt 대통령은 부자들 (moneyed interests)이 이용한 사람.

remarks about that. Well-preserved, they say. But he sits in the dark, alone, smoking, staring straight ahead of him, unblinking, into the small hours of the night.[10]

If it is as he says, if it is restful, I will let it go at that. But suppose it is not.

Suppose it is something I cannot fathom. Perhaps he needs help. Why doesn't he speak? Why doesn't he frown or laugh or cry? Why doesn't he do something? Why does he just sit there?

II

Finally I become angry. Maybe it is just my unsatisfied curiosity. Maybe I am a bit worried. Anyway, I become angry.

"Is something wrong, Pop?"

"Nothing, son. Nothing at all."

But this time I am determined not to be put off. I am angry.

"Then why do you sit here all alone, thinking, till late?"

"It's restful, son. I like it."

I am getting nowhere.[11] Tomorrow he will be sitting there again. I will be puzzled. I will be worried. I will not stop now. I am angry.

---

10) 자정을 지나 1~3시 정도까지의 시간.
11) I am getting nowhere. 점점 더 오리무중.

"Well, what do you think about, Pa? Why do you just sit here? What's worrying you? What do you think about?"

"Nothing's worrying me, son. I'm all right. It's just restful. That's all. Go to bed, son."

My anger has left me. But the feeling of worry is still there. I must get an answer. It seems so silly. Why doesn't he tell me? I have a funny feeling that unless I get an answer I will go crazy. I am insistent.

"But what do you think about, Pa? What is it?"

"Nothing, son. Just things in general. Nothing special. Just things."

I can get no answer.

It is very late. The street is quiet and the house is dark. I climb the steps softly, skipping the ones that creak. I let myself in with my key and tiptoe into my room. I remove my clothes and remember that I am thirsty. In my bare feet I walk to the kitchen. Before I reach it I know he is there.

I can see the deeper darkness of his hunched shape. He is sitting in the same chair, his elbows on his knees, his cold pipe in his teeth, his unblinking eyes staring straight ahead. He does not hear me come in. I stand quietly in the doorway and watch him.

Everything is quiet, but the night is full of little sounds. As I stand there motionless I begin to notice them. The ticking of the alarm clock on the icebox. The low hum of an automobile passing many blocks away. The swish of papers moved along the street by the breeze. A whispering rise and fall of sound, like low breathing. It is strangely pleasant.

The dryness in my throat reminds me. I step briskly into the kitchen.

"Hello, Pop." I say.

"Hello, son." he says. His voice is low and dreamlike. He does not change his position or shift his gaze.

I cannot find the faucet. The dim shadow of light that comes through the window from the street lamp only makes the room seem darker. I reach for the short chain in the center of the room. I snap on the light.

He straightens up with a jerk, as though he has been struck. "What's the matter, Pop?" I ask.

"Nothing." he says. " I don't like the light."

"What's the matter with the light?" I say. "What's wrong?"

"Nothing." he says. " I don't like the light."

I snap the light off. I drink my water slowly. I must take it easy. I say to myself. I must get to the bottom of this.

"Why don't you go to bed? Why do you sit here so late in the dark?"

" It's nice." he says. "I can't get used to lights. We didn't have lights when I was a boy in Europe."

My heart skips a beat[12] and I catch my breath happily. I

begin to think I understand. I remember the stories of his boyhood in Austria. I see the wide-beamed kretchma,13) with my grandfather behind the bar. It is late, the customers are gone, and he is dozing. I see the bed of glowing coals, the last of the roaring fire. The room is already dark, and growing darker. I see a small boy, crouched on a pile of twigs at one side of the huge fireplace, his starry gaze fixed on the dull remains of the dead flames. The boy is my father.

I remember the pleasure of those few moments while I stood quietly in the doorway watching him.

"You mean there's nothing wrong? You just sit in the dark because you like it, Pop?" I find it hard to keep my voice from rising in a happy shout.

"Sure." he says. " I can't think with the light on."

I set my glass down and turn to go back to my room. "Good night, Pop." I say.

"Good night." he says.

Then I remember. I turn back. "What do you think about, Pop?" I ask.

His voice seems to come from far away. It is quiet and even again. "Nothing." he says softly. "Nothing special."

---

12) My hearts skips a beat. 심장이 한 박자 건너뛴다. 즉 갑자기 고동친다.
13) kretchma. 난로

Comprehension Check-Up Questions

1. According to the son, what "peculiar habit" does his father have? And why does he have such habit?

2. In the story, the son reveals himself as much as the father. What kind of personality do you assume he has?

3. The story is narrated in interior monologue style. In what respects is this technique effective?

4. What relationship do you think the narrator has with other family such as the mother and the sister?

5. How do you guess the family's economic status is? What is the evidence of your guess?

6. Do you have any experience that you found some unfamiliar aspects of your family or friends? What emotions did such finding arouse you?

The Chaser

John Collier

John Henry Noyes Collier (1901-1980) was a British-born author and screenwriter best known for his short stories, many of which appeared in The New Yorker from the 1930s to the 1950s. Most were collected in *The John Collier Reader* (1972); earlier collections include a 1951 volume, the famous "Fancies and Goodnights." which won the International Fantasy Award. Individual stories are frequently anthologized in fantasy collections. John Collier's writing has been praised by authors such as Anthony Burgess, Ray Bradbury, Roald Dahl, Neil Gaiman, Michael Chabon, Wyndham Lewis, and Paul Theroux.

Words and Phrases

creaky	
obscurely	imperceptible
mixture	love-potion
stock	permanent
laxative	carnal
teething mixture	indifference
varied	neglect
beverage	better-off

I

Alan Austen, as nervous as a kitten, went up certain dark and creaky stairs in the neighbourhood of Pell Street,[1] and peered about for a long time on the dim landing before he found the name he wanted written obscurely on one of the doors.

He pushed open this door, as he had been told to do, and found himself in a tiny room, which contained no furniture but a plain kitchen table, a rocking chair, and an ordinary chair. On one of the dirty walls were a couple of shelves, containing in all[2] perhaps a dozen bottles and jars.

An old man sat in the rocking chair, reading a newspaper. Alan, without a word, handed him the card[3] he had been given.

"Sit down, Mr Austen."said the old many very politely. "I am glad to make your acquaintance."

"Is it true." asked Alan, "that you have a certain mixture that has __ er __ quite extraordinary effects?"

"My dear sir." replied the old man, "my stock in trade is not very large __ I don't deal in laxatives and teething mixtures __ but it is varied. I think nothing I sell has effects which could be described as ordinary."[4]

---

1) a principal street in New York's Chinatown.
2) in all: altogether: 모두 합쳐서.
3) the card: the name card.
4) nothing I sell has effects which could be described as ordinary: 내가 판매하는 것 어느

"Well, the fact is __" began Alan.

"Here, for example." interrupted the old man, reaching for a bottle from the shelf. "Here is a liquid as colourless as water, almost tasteless, quite imperceptible in coffee, milk, wine, or any other beverage. It is also quite imperceptible to any known method of autopsy."

"Do you mean it is a poison?" cried Alan, very much horrified.

"Call it cleaning fluid if you like." said the old man indifferently. "Lives[5] need cleaning. Call it spot-remover. 'Out, damned spot!' Eh? 'Out, brief candle!'"

"I want nothing of that sort." said Alan.

"Probably it is just as well." said the old man. "Do you know the price of this? For one teaspoonful, which is sufficient, I ask five thousand dollars. Never less, Not a penny less."

"I hope all you mixtures are not as expensive." said Alan apprehensively.

"Oh, dear, no." said the old man. "It would be no good charging in that sort of price for a love-potion, for example. Young people who need a love-potion very seldom have five thousand dollars. If they had[6] they would not need a love-potion."

"I look at it like this."[7] said the old man. "Please a customer

---

것도 ordinary하다고 표현할 만한 것은 없어요. 내가 파는 물건은 모두가 extraordinary하다.

5) 여기서는 life의 복수형으로 need의 주어.

6) if they had five thousand dollars.

7) 나는 이렇게 보죠. this는 뒤에 나오는 문장. it는 비인칭으로 상황을 가리킴.

with one article, and he will come back when he needs another.[8)]
Even if it is more costly, he will save up for it, if necessary."

II

"So." said Alan, "you really do sell love-potions?"

"If I did not sell love-potions."[9)] said the old man, "I should
not have mentioned the other matter to you."

"And these potions." said Alan. "They are not just __ just __
er __"[10)]

"Oh, no." said the old man. "Their effects are permanent, and
extend far beyond the mere carnal impulse. But they include it.
Oh, yes, they include it. Bountifully, Insistently. Everlastingly."

"Dear me!" said Alan, "How very interesting!"

"Consider the spiritual side, too" said the old man.

"I do, indeed." said Alan.

"For indifference." said the old man, "They substitute
devotion. For scorn, adoration. Give one tiny measure of this to
the young lady __ its flavour is imperceptible in orange juice,
soup, or cocktails __ and however gay and giddy she is, she will

---

8) 고객을 하나의 물품으로 감동시켜라. 그러면 반드시 그 다음 물건이 필요할 때 다시 올 것이다.
   명령문 ~ and의 용법으로 if ~ 와 동일한 의미.

9) 이하 주절과 함께 가정법 시제. 사랑의 묘약이 없다면, 다른 물건 소개도 안했을 것이요. 주절의
   the other matter는 다른 것, 즉 life cleaner.

10) Alan은 love potion의 효력이 일시적이거나 육체적인 것에만 국한되지나 않을까 주저함. 이어지는
   old man의 설명은 묘약이 육체적인 사랑과 함께 정신적 사랑 모두를 영원히 얻는 약이라고 강조함.

change altogether. She'll want nothing but solitude, and you."

"I can hardly believe it." said Alan. "She is so fond of parties."

"She will not like them anymore." said the old man. "She'll be afraid of the pretty girls you may meet."

"She'll actually be jealous?" cried Alan in a rapture. "Of me?"

"Yes, she'll want to be everything to you."

"She is already. Only she doesn't care about it."

"She will, when she has taken this. She will care intensely. You'll be her sole interest in life."

"Wonderful!" cried Alan.

"She'll want to know all you do." said the old man. "All that has happened to you during the day. Every word of it. She'll want to know what you are thinking about, why you smile suddenly, why you are looking sad."

"That is love!" said Alan.

"Yes." said the old man. "How carefully she'll look after you! She'll never allow you to be tired nor to neglect your food. If you are an hour late, she'll be terrified. She'll think you are killed, or that some Siren[11] has caught you."

"I can hardly imagine Diana like that!" cried Alan, overwhelmed with joy.

"You will not have to use your imagination." said the old

---

11) Siren: a reference to the minor goddesses of Greek mythology who lived on an island and used their enchanting voices to lure sailors to their death upon the rocks. 여기서는 사이렌과 같이 유혹하는 여성.

man. "And, by the way, since there are always sirens, if by chance you should, later on, slip a little, you need not worry. She will forgive you, in the end. She'll be terribly hurt, of course, but she'll forgive __ in the end."

"That will not happen." said Alan fervently.

"Of course not." said the old man. "But, if it does, you need not worry. She'll never divorce you. Oh, no! And, of course, she herself will never give you the least, the very least, grounds for divorce, of course."

"And how much." said Alan, "how much is this wonderful mixture?"

"It is not as expensive." said the old man, "as the spot-remover, as I think we agreed to call it. No. That[12) is five thousand dollars; never a penny less. One has to be older than you are to indulge in that sort of thing. One has to save up for it."

"But the love-potion?" said Alan.

"Oh, that." said the old man, opening the drawer in the kitchen table and taking out a tiny, rather dirty-looking bottle. "That is just a dollar."

"I can't tell you how grateful I am." said Alan, watching him fill it.

"I like to help my customers." said the old man. "Then they come back later in life, when they are rather better-off, and want more

---

12) spot-remover.

expensive things. Here you are. You will find it very effective."

"Thank you again." said Alan. "Good-bye."

"Au revoir."[13] said the old man.

---

13) (French) Good-bye until we meet again.

1. Describe the personalities of the characters. Give some evidences to support your idea. (Alan, the old man, Diana)

2. Do you think Alan might come back to the shop in the future? If yes, for what purpose?

3. How confident is the old man of Alan's revisiting? And what do you guess makes him so confident?

4. What is the theme or lesson of the story?

5. Explain the tone of the story.

6. What is the meaning of the title, "the Chaser"?

7. Explain the irony of the story.

Charles

Shirley Hardie Jackson

Shirley Hardie Jackson (1916–1965) was an American writer, known primarily for her works of horror and mystery. Over the duration of her writing career, which spanned over two decades, she composed six novels, two memoirs, and over 200 short stories.

Born in San Francisco, California, Jackson later attended Syracuse University in New York, where she became involved with the university's literary magazine and met her future husband Stanley Edgar Hyman. The couple settled in North Bennington, Vermont in 1940, after which Hyman established a career as a literary critic, and Jackson began writing. After publishing her debut novel *The Road Through the Wall* (1948), a semi-autobiographical account of her childhood in California, Jackson gained significant public attention for her short story "The Lottery", which details a secret, sinister underside to a bucolic American village. She continued to publish numerous short stories in literary journals and magazines throughout the 1950s, some of which were assembled and reissued in her 1953 memoir *Life Among the Savages*. In 1959, she published *The Haunting of Hill House*, a supernatural horror novel widely considered to be one of the best ghost stories ever written.

I

The day my son Laurie started kindergarten he renounced corduroy overalls with bibs and began wearing blue jeans with a belt[1]; I watched him go off the first morning with the older girl

---

[1] he renounced corduroy overalls with bibs and began wearing blue jeans with a belt bib(턱받이; (에이프런 따위의) 가슴 부분)가 달린 골덴 overall(아래 위가 달린 통옷, 통바지)을 거부하고 벨트 달린 청바지를 입기 시작했다.

next door, seeing clearly that an era of my life was ended, my sweet-voiced nursery-school tot replaced by a long-trousered, swaggering character[2] who forgot to stop at the corner and wave good-bye to me.

He came home the same way the front door slamming open, his cap on the floor[3], and the voice suddenly become raucous shouting, "Isn't anybody here?"

At lunch he spoke insolently to his father, spilled his baby sister's milk, and remarked that his teacher said we were not to take the name of the Lord in vain.

"How was school today?" I asked, elaborately casual.[4]

"All right." he said.

"Did you learn anything?" his father asked.

Laurie regarded his father coldly, "I didn't learn nothing." he said.

"Anything." I said. "Didn't learn anything."

"The teacher spanked a boy though." Laurie said, addressing his bread and butter.[5] "For being fresh."[6] he added, with his

---

2) my sweet-voiced nursery-school tot (being) replaced by a long-trousered, swaggering character 분사구문 문장. 달콤한 목소리의 유아원 아이가 긴 바지의 으스대는 (유치원생) 아이로 바뀌었다.

3) the front door slamming open, his cap on the floor. 분사구문 문장. 현관문이 활짝 열리며, 모자가 마루바닥에. (던져지면서)

4) (being) elaborately casual. 분사구문 애써 캐주얼하면서. 즉 아슬아슬하게 무례한 아들의 행동에 대해 애써 모르는 척 대하면서.

5) addressing bread and butter. 분사구문. 버터빵을 먹으며. address는 음식을 먹기 시작하다.

6) fresh. 무례한.

mouth full.

"What did he do?" I asked. "Who was it?"

Laurie thought. "It was Charles." he said. "He was fresh. The teacher spanked him and made him stand in a corner. He was awfully fresh."

What did he do?" I asked again, but Laurie slid off his chair, took a cookie, and left, while his father was still saying, "See here, young man."

The next day Laurie remarked at lunch, as soon as he sat down, "Well, Charles was bad again today." He grinned enormously and said, "Today Charles hit the teacher."

"Good heavens." I said, mindful of the Lord's name, "I suppose he got spanked again?"

"He sure did." Laurie said. "Look up." he said to his father.

"What?" his father said, looking up.

"Look down." Laurie said. "Look at my thumb. Gee, you're dumb." He began to laugh insanely. "Why did Charles hit the teacher?" I asked quickly.

"Because she tried to make him color with red crayons." Laurie said. "Charles wanted to color with green crayons so he hit the teacher and she spanked him and said nobody play with Charles but everybody did."

The third day ___ it was Wednesday of the first week ___ Charles bounced a see-saw onto the head of a little girl and made her bleed, and the teacher made him stay inside all during recess.

Thursday Charles had to stand in a corner during story-time because he kept pounding his feet on the floor. Friday Charles was deprived of blackboard privileges[7] because he threw chalk.

On Saturday I remarked to my husband, "Do you think kindergarten is too unsettling[8] for Laurie? All this toughness, and bad grammar, and this Charles boy sounds like such a bad influence."

"It'll be all right." my husband said reassuringly, "Bound to be people like Charles[9] in the world. Might as well meet them now as later."[10]

II

On Monday Laurie came home late, full of news. "Charles." he shouted as he came up the hill; I was waiting anxiously on the front steps. "Charles." Laurie yelled all the way up the hill, "Charles was bad again."

---

7) blackboard privileges 칠판을 사용할 권리.

8) unsettling 불안정한.

9) bound to be people like Charles. 찰스같은 사람이 있게 마련이다. 주어 there are 생략.

10) Might as well meet them now as later. 그런 사람(찰스같은 사람)을 지금 만나는 것도 괜찮지. might as well ~하는 것도 괜찮다.

"Come right in." I said, as soon as he came close enough. "Lunch is waiting."

"You know what Charles did?" he demanded, following me through the door. "Charles yelled so in school they sent a boy in from first grade to tell the teacher she had to make Charles keep quiet,11) and so Charles had to stay after school. And so all the children stayed to watch him."

"What did he do?" I asked.

"He just sat there." Laurie said, climbing into his chair at the table. "Hi, Pop, y'old dust mop."

"Charles had to stay after school today" I told my husband. "Everyone stayed with him."

"What does this Charles look like?" my husband asked Laurie. "What's his other name?"

"He's bigger than me." Laurie said. "And he doesn't have any rubbers and he doesn't ever wear a jacket."

Monday night was the first Parent-Teachers meeting,12) and only the fact that the baby had a cold kept me from going; I wanted passionately to meet Charles's mother. On Tuesday Laurie remarked suddenly "Our teacher had a friend come to

---

11) Charles yelled so in school (that) they sent a boy in from frist grade to tell the teacher she had to make Charles keep quiet. so that 구문. 학교에서 찰스가 하도 소리를 질러 they(학교일을 보는 일반적 사람, 교사 누군가)가 1학년 교실로부터 한 소년을 보냈다. 선생님이 찰스를 조용히 시키라고 말하러.

12) Parent-Teachers meeting. 교사 학부모 모임. Parent-Teachers Association이라고 하며 P.T.A.로 약칭함.

see her in school today."

"Charles's mother?" my husband and I asked simultaneously.

"Naaah."[13] Laurie said scornfully, "It was a man who came and made us do exercises, we had to touch our toes. Look." He climbed down from his chair and squatted down and touched his toes. "Like this." he said. He got solemnly back into his chair and said, picking up his fork, "Charles didn't even do exercises."

"That's fine." I said heartily, "Didn't Charles want to do exercises?"

"Naaah." Laurie said. "Charles was so fresh to the teacher's friend he wasn't let do exercises."[14]

"Fresh again?" I said.

"He kicked the teacher's friend." Laurie said. "The teacher's friend told Charles to touch his toes like I just did and Charles kicked him."

"What are they going to do about Charles, do you suppose?" Laurie's father asked him.

Laurie shrugged elaborately, "Throw him out of school, I guess." he said.

Wednesday and Thursday were routine[15]; Charles yelled

---

13) Naaah. "No"를 다소 건들거리며 발음함.

14) Charles was so fresh to the teacher's friend (that) he wasn't let do exercise. so that 구문. he wasn't let do exercise는 the teacher's friend did not let him(Charles) do exercise의 수동태꼴. 따라서 더 문법적으로 바른 문장은 "to"가 살아난, he wasn't let to do exercise임.

15) routine 일상. 반복되는 일상. 챨스가 늘 fresh한 행동을 하는 일상들.

during story hour and hit a boy in the stomach and made him cry, On Friday Charles stayed after school again and so did all the other children.

With the third week of kindergarten Charles was an institution[16] in our family; the baby was being a Charles when she cried all afternoon; Laurie did a Charles when he filled his wagon full of mud and pulled it through the kitchen; even my husband, when he caught his elbow in the telephone cord and pulled telephone, ashtray and a bowl of flowers off the table, said, after the first minute, "Looks like Charles."

During the third and fourth weeks it looked like a reformation[17] in Charles; Laurie reported grimly at lunch on Thursday of the third week, "Charles was so good today the teacher gave him an apple."

"What?" I said, and my husband added warily "You mean Charles?"

"Charles." Laurie said. "He gave the crayons around and he picked up the books afterward and the teacher said he was her helper."

"What happened?" I asked incredulously,

"He was her helper, that's all." Laurie said, and shrugged.

"Can this be true, about Charles?" I asked my husband that

---

16) institution. 하나의 정착된 관례 혹은 관례적 표현.
17) reformation. 혁명. 챨스의 행동의 변화가 하나의 혁명처럼 급전했음을 의미.

night. "Can something like this happen?"

"Wait and see." my husband said cynically, "When you've got a Charles to deal with, this may mean he's only plotting."[18]

He seemed to be wrong. For over a week. Charles was the , teacher's helper; each day he handed things out and he picked things up; no one had to stay after school.

"The P.T.A. meeting's next week again." I told my husband one evening. "I'm going to find Charles's mother there."

"Ask her what happened to Charles." my husband said. "I'd like to know."

"I'd like to know myself." I said.

On Friday of that week things were back to normal. "You know what Charles did today?" Laurie demanded at the lunch table, in a voice slightly awed. "He told a little girl to say a word and she said it and the teacher washed her mouth out with soap and Charles laughed."

"What word?" his father asked unwisely and Laurie said, "I'll have to whisper it to you, it's so bad." He got down off his chair and went around to his father. His father bent his head down and Laurie whispered joyfully, His father's eyes widened.

"Did Charles tell the little girl to say that?" he asked respectfully,

---

18) When you've got a Charles to deal with, this may mean he's only plotting. 찰스 같은 아이를 상대할 때에는, 이 일(갑자기 착하게 된 일)이 뭔가 음모를 꾸미고 있다는 뜻이 될 수도 있다. Charles 앞에 a가 붙은 것에 유의.

"She said it twice." Laurie said. "Charles told her to say it twice."

"What happened to Charles?" my husband asked.

"Nothing." Laurie said. "He was passing out the crayons."

III

Monday morning Charles abandoned the little girl[19] and said the evil word himself three or four times, getting his mouth washed out with soap each time. He also threw chalk.

My husband came to the door with me that evening as I set out for the P.T.A. meeting.

"Invite her over for a cup of tea after the meeting." he said. "I want to get a look at her."

"If only she's there." I said prayerfully,

"She'll be there." my husband said. "I don't see how they could hold a P.T.A. meeting without Charles's mother."

At the meeting I sat restlessly scanning each comfortable matronly face, trying to determine which one hid the secret of Charles. None of them looked to me haggard enough. No one stood up in the meeting and apologized for the way her son had been acting. No one mentioned Charles.

---

19) abandoned the little girl. 그 여자 아이를 포기하고. 즉 여자 아이를 시켜 bad word를 대신 말하게 하는 작전을 버리고 자기가 직접 말하는 방법 선택.

After the meeting I identified and sought out Laurie's kindergarten teacher. She had a plate with a cup of tea and a piece of chocolate cake; I had a plate with a cup of tea and a piece of marshmallow cake. We maneuvered up to one another cautiously; and smiled.

"I've been so anxious to meet you." I said. "I'm Laurie's mother."

"We're all so interested in Laurie." she said.

"Well, he certainly likes kindergarten." I said. "He talks about it all the time."

"We had a little trouble adjusting, the first week or so." she said primly "but now he's a fine little helper. With occasional lapses, of course."

"Laurie usually adjusts very quickly" I said. "I suppose this time it's Charles's influence."

"Charles?"

"Yes." I said laughing, "you must have your hands full in that kindergarten, with Charles."

"Charles?" she said. "We don't have any Charles in the kindergarten."

Comprehension Check-Up Questions

1. Explain in detail how Laurie changes as he starts his kindergarten.

2. List the bad behaviors Charles commits in the school every week.

3. What kind of personality do you think Laurie's parents have? Why do you think so?

4. What do the parents think about their son and how do they think the kindergarten affects him?

5. Why does the mother miss the first P.T.A?

6. Explain Charles' transformation in the third and forth weeks.

7. What does the mother find in the end?

Desiree's Baby

Kate Chopin

Kate Chopin (/ˈʃoʊpæn/;1850–1904) was an American author of short stories and novels based in Louisiana. She is now considered by some scholars to have been a forerunner of American 20th-century feminist authors.

Of maternal French and paternal Irish descent, Chopin was born in St. Louis, Missouri. She married and moved with her husband to New Orleans. They later lived in the country in Cloutierville, Louisiana. From 1892 to 1895, Chopin wrote short stories for both children and adults that were published in several noted magazines. Her stories aroused controversy because of her subjects and her approach; they were condemned as immoral by some critics. Her major works were two short story collections: *Bayou Folk* (1894) and *A Night in Acadie* (1897). Her important short stories included "Désirée's Baby" (1893), a tale of miscegenation in antebellum Louisiana, "The Story of an Hour"(1894), and "The Storm" (1898). Chopin also wrote two novels: *At Fault* (1890) and *The Awakening* (1899). Within a decade of her death, Chopin was widely recognized as one of the leading writers of her time.

pillar	steep
dada: daddy	cowl
toddling age	galleries
speculation	encircle
affection	thick-leaved
pistol shot	far-reaching branches
avalanche	strict master
prairie fire	easy-going
drive headlong	indulgent
corbeille	full length
patience	deafening
shudder	account for
gentle presence of a mistress	averted eyes
plantation	cradle of willow
deserted field	dainty decorations
stubble	layette
bayou	espousal
bonfire	remnant

I

As the day was pleasant, Madame Valmonde drove over to L'Abri[1] to see Desiree and the baby.

It made her laugh to think of Desiree with a baby. Why, it seemed only yesterday that Desiree was little more than a baby herself; when Monsieur in riding through the gateway of Valmonde[2] had found her lying asleep in the shadow of the big stone pillar.

The little one awoke in his arms and began to cry for "Dada." Some people thought she might have strayed there of her own accord,[3] for she was of the toddling age. However, most people believed that she had been purposely left by somebody. Soon Madame Valmonde abandoned every speculation except the one that Desiree had been sent to her by a beneficent Providence[4] to be the child of her affection, seeing that she was without her own child of the flesh. The girl grew to be beautiful and gentle, affectionate and sincere and became the idol of the Valmondes.

It was no wonder, when she stood one day against the stone pillar in whose shadow she had lain asleep eighteen years before, that Armand Aubigny riding by and seeing her there,

---

1) L'Abri: Aubigny의 집. Desiree와 그 남편인 Armand Aubigny가 사는 집.
2) when Monsieur in riding through the gateway of Valmonde: 발몽 저택의 대문으로 말을 타고 들어오던 무슈 발몽(마담 발몽의 남편)이.
3) of her own accord: 스스로/혼자힘으로.
4) Providence: God.

had fallen in love with her. That was the way all the Aubignys[5] fell in love, as if struck by a pistol shot. In fact, he had known her since his father brought him home from Paris, a boy of eight, after his mother died there. However, it was the day that he felt love for her. The passion that awoke in him that day, when he saw her at the gate, swept along like an avalanche, or like a prairie fire, or like anything that drives headlong over all obstacles.

Monsieur Valmonde was practical and wanted things well considered: that is, the girl's obscure origin.[6] Armand looked into her eyes and did not care. He was reminded that she was nameless. What did it matter about a name when he could give her one of the oldest and proudest in Louisiana?[7] He ordered the corbeille from Paris, and contained himself with all his patience until it arrived; then they were married.

---

5) Aubigny 가문의 사람들.

6) Monsieur Valmonde was practical and wanted things well considered: that is, the girl's obscure origin Valmonde씨는 현실적인 남자라서 모든 일이 먼저 잘 숙고되어야 한다고 보았다/ 즉, Desiree의 출생에 대해 결혼 전에 Armand에게 한 번 더 확실히 상기시켜 줌.

7) What did it matter about a name when he could give her one of the oldest and proudest in Louisiana? 루이지애나에서 최고로 전통있고 자랑스러운 이름_ 즉 Mrs.Aubigny_을 이제 물려줄 수 있게 되는데 nameless하다는 사실이 대수냐?

II

Madame Valmonde had not seen Desiree and the baby for four weeks. When she reached L'Abri[8] she shuddered at the first sight of it, as she always did. It was a sad looking place, which for many years had not known the gentle presence of a mistress. Old Monsieur Aubigny[9] had married and buried his wife in France; she loved France, her own land, too much to leave it.

The roof came down steep and black like a cowl, reaching out beyond the wide galleries that encircled the yellow stuccoed house.[10] Big, solemn oaks grew close to it, and their thick-leaved, far-reaching branches shadowed it like a pall. Young Aubigny was such a strict master that his slaves had forgotten to be joyful. They had been joyful during the old master's easy-going and indulgent lifetime.

Desiree was recovering slowly, and lay full length, in her soft white muslins and laces, upon a couch. The baby was beside her, upon her arm, where he had fallen asleep, at her breast. The yellow nurse woman[11] sat beside a window fanning herself.

---

8) L'Abri: Aubigny의 집.
9) Old Monsieur Aubigny: Armand의 아버지.
10) 노란 벽토로 치장된 집을 빙 둘러싼 회랑.
11) The yellow nurse woman: 흑백 혼혈인 유모. 이 시대는 아직 노예해방 이전의 시대이며 흑인의 피가 조금이라도 섞였으면 모두 흑인으로 간주하여 노예로 취급.

Madame Valmonde bent over Desiree and kissed her, holding her an instant tenderly in her arms. Then she turned to the child.

"This is not the baby!" she exclaimed, in startled tones. She said it in French. French was the language spoken at Valmonde in those days.

"I knew you would be astonished." laughed Desiree, "at the way he has grown. Look at his legs, mamma, and his hands and fingernails __ real fingernails. Zandrine had to cut them this morning. Isn't it true, Zandrine?"

The nurse woman bowed her head majestically, "Mais si, Madame."

"And the way he cries." went on Desiree, "is deafening. Armand heard him the other day as far away as La Blanche's cabin."[12]

Madame Valmonde had never removed her eyes from the child. She lifted the baby and walked with it over to the window that was lightest. She scanned the baby narrowly,[13] then looked as searchingly[14] at Zandrine, but Zandrine turned her face to the outside.

"Yes, the child has grown, has changed." said Madame

---

12) 블랑쉬의 오두막. 블랑쉬는 white를 뜻하는 불어. 피부색이 백인처럼 하얗지만 그래도 흑인의 피가 섞여 있어서 블랑쉬 역시 노예 여성임. Zandrine이나 블랑쉬처럼 피부색이 밝은 여성 노예 는 들일 대신 주인의 가정집에서 요리사나 유모 등의 일을 하였다.

13) narrowly: 주의 깊게.

14) as searchingly: 뭔가를 물어보려는 듯이.

Valmonde, slowly, as she replaced it beside its mother. "What does Armand say?"

Desiree's face became suffused with a glow that was happiness itself.

"Oh, Armand is the proudest father in the world, I believe, chiefly because it is a boy, to bear his name; though he says that he would have loved a girl as well. But I know it isn't true. I know he says that to please me. And mamma." she added, drawing Madame Valmonde's head down to her, and speaking in a whisper, "he hasn't punished one of the slaves __ not one of them __ since baby is born. Even at Negrillon, who pretended to have burnt his leg so that he might rest from work __ he only laughed, and said Negrillon was a great scamp. Oh, mamma, I'm so happy."

What Desiree said was true. Marriage, and later the birth of his son had softened Armand Aubigny's imperious and exacting nature[15] very much. This was what made the gentle Desiree so happy, for she loved him desperately. When he frowned she trembled, but loved him. When he smiled, she asked no greater blessing of God. But Armand's dark, handsome face had not often been disfigured by frowns since the day he fell in love with her.

---

15) imperious and exacting nature: 제왕 같고 엄정한 성격.

III

When the baby was about three months old, Desiree awoke one day to the conviction that there was something in the air menacing her peace.[16] It was at first too subtle to grasp. It had only been a disquieting suggestion; an air of mystery among the black slaves; unexpected visits from far-off neighbors who could hardly account for their coming. Then a strange, an awful change in her husband's manner, which she dared not ask him to explain. When he spoke to her, it was with averted eyes, from which the old love-light seemed to have gone out. He absented himself from home; and even when he was home, he avoided her and the baby, without any explanation. And the very spirit of Satan seemed suddenly to take hold of him in his dealings with the slaves. Desiree was miserable enough to die.

She sat in her room, one hot afternoon, in her peignoir,[17] listlessly drawing through her fingers the strands of her long, silky brown hair that hung about her shoulders. The baby, half naked, lay asleep upon her own great mahogany bed. One little quadroon boy[18] __ half naked too __ stood fanning the baby slowly with a fan of peacock feathers. Desiree's eyes had been

---

16) awoke one day to the conviction that there was something in the air menacing her peace: 평화를 위협하는 뭔가를 주변 분위기 속에서 확연히 느끼게 됨.

17) peignoir: 실내복.

18) quadroon: 백인과 반백인과의 혼혈아/4분의 1 백인.

fixed absently and sadly upon the baby, while she was striving to penetrate the threatening mist that she felt closing about her.[19] She looked from her child to the boy who stood beside him, and back again; over and over. "Ah!" It was a cry that she could not help; which she was not conscious of having uttered. Her blood turned like ice in her veins, and a clammy moisture[20] gathered upon her face.

She tried to speak to the little quadroon boy; but no sound would come, at first. When the boy heard his name uttered, he looked up, and his mistress was pointing to the door. He laid aside the great, soft fan, and obediently stole away,[21] over the polished floor, on his bare tiptoes.

She stayed motionless, with gaze riveted upon her child,[22] and her face was full of fright.

At the moment her husband entered the room, and without noticing her, went to a table and began to search among some papers which covered it.

"Armand." she called to him, in a voice which must have stabbed him. But he did not notice. "Armand." she said again. Then she rose and tottered towards him. "Armand." she panted

---

19) while she was striving to penetrate the threatening mist that she felt closing about her: 자신 주위에서 자신을 엄습하는 위협적인 분위기가 무엇인지를 알려고 애쓰면서.
20) a clammy moisture: 끈적끈적한 수분/진땀.
21) stole away: 살금살금 걷다.
22) 아기에게 눈을 떼지 못한 채.

once more, clutching his arm, "look at our child. What does it mean? Tell me."

He coldly but gently loosened her fingers from about his arm and thrust the hand away from him. "Tell me what it means!" she cried despairingly.

"It means." he answered lightly, "that the child is not white; it means that you are not white."

"It is a lie; it is not true, I am white! Look at my hair, it is brown; and my eyes are gray, Armand, you know they are gray. And my skin is white." seizing his wrist. "Look at my hand; whiter than yours, Armand." she laughed hysterically.

"As white as La Blanche's." he returned cruelly; and went away leaving her alone with their child.

When she could hold a pen in her hand, she sent a despairing letter to Madame Valmonde.

"My mother, they tell me I am not white. Armand has told me I am not white. For God's sake tell them it is not true. You must know it is not true. I shall die. I must die. I cannot be so unhappy, and live."

The answer that came was brief:

"My own Desiree: Come home to Valmonde; back to your mother who loves you. Come with your child."

When the letter reached Desiree she went with it to her husband's study, and laid it open upon the desk. She was like a stone image: silent, white, motionless after she placed it there.

In silence he ran his cold eyes over the written words.

He said nothing. "Shall I go, Armand?" she asked in tones sharp with agonized suspense.

"Yes, go."

"Do you want me to go?"

"Yes, I want you to go."

He thought Almighty God had dealt cruelly and unjustly with him; and felt, somehow, that he was paying Him back when he stabbed thus into his wife's soul. Moreover he no longer loved her, because of the unconscious injury she had brought upon his home and his name.

She turned away like one stunned by a blow, and walked slowly towards the door, hoping he would call her back.

"Good-by, Armand." she moaned.

He did not answer her. That was his last blow at fate.[23]

Desiree went in search of her child. Zandrine was pacing the gallery with the child. She took the little one from the nurse's arms with no word of explanation, and descending the steps, walked away, under the oak branches.

It was an October afternoon; the sun was just sinking. Out in the still fields the negroes were picking cotton.

Desiree had not changed the thin white garment nor the slippers which she wore.[24] Her hair was uncovered and the

---

23) his last blow at fate: 운명에 가하는 그의 마지막 일격.

sun's rays brought a golden gleam from its brown meshes. She did not take the broad, beaten road[25] which led to the far-off plantation of Valmonde. She walked across a deserted field, where the stubble bruised her tender feet and tore her thin gown to shreds.

She disappeared among the reeds and willows that grew thick along the banks of the deep, sluggish bayou; and she did not come back again.

VI

Some weeks later there was a strange scene at L'Abri. In the centre of the smoothly swept back yard was a great bonfire,[26] Armand Aubigny sat in the wide hallway watching the spectacle of the bonfire; and it was he who gave to a half dozen negroes the material which kept this fire ablaze.

A graceful cradle of willow, with all its dainty decorations, was laid upon the fire, which had already been fed with the richness of a expensive layette. Then there were silk gowns, and velvet and satin ones added to these; laces, too, and embroideries;

---

24) Desiree had not changed the thin white garment nor the slippers which she wore
 : 실내복과 신고 있던 슬리퍼 차림으로 집을 나옴.
25) the broad, beaten road: 사람이 많이 다니는 넓은 길.
26) 잔디를 곱게 깎은 뒤뜰에 큰 모닥불을 지펴놓음.

bonnets and gloves; for the corbeille had been of rare quality.

The last thing to go was a tiny bundle of letters; innocent little scribblings that Desiree had sent to him during the days of their espousal. There was the remnant of one back in the drawer from which he took them. But it was not Desiree's; it was part of an old letter from his mother to his father. He read it. She was thanking God for the blessing of her husband's love:

"But above all," she wrote, "night and day, I thank the good God for having so arranged our lives that our dear Armand will never know that his mother, who adores him, belongs to the race that is cursed with the brand of slavery."

Comprehension Check-Up Questions

1. Where had Mr.Valmonde found Desiree for the first time? And why did the Valmondes adopt her?

2. How did Armand fall in love with Desiree? And how did he receive her origins?

3. How old was Desiree's baby when her mother visited?

4. How did Armand's house look like?

5. How was Armand different from his father?

6. How did Desiree feel about her baby and marriage?

7. How did Armand change after the baby was born?

8. Who's fanning beside the baby sleeping?

9. What did "the mystery" turn out?

10. How did Armand explain about the baby mixed?

11. What was Madame Valmonds' reply to Desiree's letter?

12. What truth turned out at the end?

A Mother in Mannville

Marjorie Rawlings

Marjorie Kinnan Rawlings (1896–1953) was an American author who lived in rural Florida and wrote novels with rural themes and settings. Her best known work, *The Yearling*, about a boy who adopts an orphaned fawn, won a Pulitzer Prize for fiction in 1939 and was later made into a movie of the same name. The book was written long before the concept of young adult fiction, but is now commonly included in teen-reading lists.

Words and Phrases

snowdrifts	clear well of his eyes
mountain peaks	gratitude
swirls down the valleys	affection
stiff	firm granite
he cookhouse	fly stoop
rhododendron	pointer
stirred the hemlocks	belated
subtropics	mountain passes

maples	treacherously
corn shocks and pumpkins	was impelled to
black walnut trees	resentment
and the lift of hills	the executives
the cabin	granted, perhaps, that s+v
undersized	contented herself
a torn shirt	with sending him skates
blunt	thistledown
annoy	a trifle abstracted
asters	relieved me of the ache
integrity.	the anomalous relation
acquaintance	imperial yellow
possess	easily duplicate
subterfuge	spinster's eyes
predicated adj.	

The orphanage is high in the Carolina mountains. Sometimes in winter the snowdrifts are so deep that the institution is cut off from the village below,[1] from all the world. Fog hides the

---

1) the snowdrifts are so deep that the institution is cut off from the village below.

mountain peaks, the snow swirls down the valleys, and a wind blows so bitterly that the orphanage boys who take the milk twice daily to the baby cottage reach the door with fingers stiff in an agony of numbness.[2]

"Or when we carry trays from the cookhouse for the ones that are sick." Jerry said, "we get our faces frostbit,[3] because we can't put our hands over them. I have gloves." he added. "Some of the boys don't have any."

He liked the late spring, he said. The rhododendron[4] was in bloom, a carpet of color, across the mountainsides, soft as the May winds that stirred the hemlocks. He called it laurel.

"It's pretty when the laurel blooms." he said. "Some of it's pink and some of it's white."

I was there in the autumn. I wanted quiet, isolation, to do some troublesome writing. I wanted mountain air to blow out

---

snowdrift휘몰아치는 눈)이 매우 깊게 몰아쳐 시설(여기서는 orphanage, 즉 보육원)은 아래 마을로부터 고립이 되어버린다.

[2] a wind blows so bitterly that the orphanage boys who take the milk twice daily to the baby cottage reach the door with fingers stiff in an agony of numbness. that 이하 절에서 주어는 the orphanage boys, 동사는 reach. stiffs는 앞의 fingers를 설명해 주는 형용사(with fingers being stiff). 바람이 혹독하게 불어서, 아기 건물로 하루에 두 번 우유를 날라주는 보육원 소년들은 무감각의 고통 속에서 뻣뻣이 굳은(stiff) 손가락을 하고서 문에 다다른다. 즉 우유를 나르는 동안 손가락이 얼어 감각이 없어진다.

[3] "Or when we carry trays from the cookhouse for the ones that are sick, we get our faces frostbit" 혹은 우리가 (소년들이) 아픈 아이들을 위해 조리실로부터 (음식) 접시를 나를 때, 우리는 얼굴이 동상 걸리게(frostbit) 되어요." get+목적어+과거분사.

[4] rhododendron 우리나라 철쭉꽃같은 모양의 꽃. Jerry는 이 꽃의 학명이 어려워 그냥 laurel(월계수)라고 부른다.

the malaria from too long a time in the subtropics.[5] I was homesick, too, for the flaming of maples in October, and for corn shocks and pumpkins and black walnut trees and the lift of hills. I found them all, living in a cabin that belonged to the orphanage, half a mile beyond the orphanage farm. When I took the cabin, I asked for a boy or man to come and chop wood for the fireplace. The first few days were warm, I found what wood I needed about the cabin, no one came, and I forgot the order.[6]

I looked up from my typewriter one late afternoon, a little startled.[7] A boy stood at the door, and my pointer dog, my companion, was at his side and had not barked to warn me. The boy was probably twelve years old, but undersized. He wore overalls and a torn shirt.

He said, "I can chop some wood today."

I said, "But I have a boy coming from the orphanage."

"I'm the boy."

"You? But you're small."

"Size don't matter, chopping wood." he said. "Some of the big

---

5) I wanted mountain air to blow out the malaria from too long a time in the subtropics. 아열대 지방에서의 너무 긴 시간으로부터 (얻은) 말라리아를 날려버리기 위해 산 공기가 필요하였다.

6) I asked for a boy or man to come and chop wood for the fireplace. The first few days were warm, I found what wood I needed about the cabin, no one came, and I forgot the order. 와서 벽난로를 위한 나무를 잘라 줄 소년이나 어른을 (보육원에) 부탁하였다. 처음 며칠은 날씨가 따뜻하였고, 집 주위에서 필요한 나무를 찾아내었으며, 아무도 (보육원에서) 오지 않았기 때문에, 난 그 부탁(the order)을 잊고 있었다.

7) a little startled. being a little startled. 분사구문. 약간 놀라서.

boys don't chop good. I've been chopping wood at the orphanage a long time."

I visualized mangled and inadequate branches for my fires.[8] I was well into my work and not inclined to conversation.[9] I was a little blunt.

"Very well. There's the ax. Go ahead and see what you can do."

I went back to work, closing the door. At first the sound of the boy dragging brush annoyed me. Then he began to chop. The blows were rhythmic and steady; and shortly I had forgotten him, the sound no more of an interruption than a consistent rain.[10] I suppose an hour and a half passed, for when I stopped and stretched, and heard the boy's steps on the cabin stoop, the sun was dropping behind the farthest mountain, and the valleys were purple with something deeper than the asters.

The boy said, "I have to go to supper now. I can come again tomorrow evening."

I said, "I'll pay you now for what you've done." thinking I should probably have to insist on an older boy, "Ten cents an hour?"

---

8) I visualized mangled and inadequate branches for my fires. 나는 나의 불을 위한 난도질되고 부적당한 나뭇가지들을 눈 앞에 떠올렸다. 제리가 제대로 된 나무를 자르지 못하고 잔가지 같은 것을 대강 잘라놓을 것이라고 생각.

9) I was well into my work and (was) not inclined to conversation. 나는 내 작업에 꽤 몰두하고 있었으며 그래서 대화의 의향이 없었다. be inclined to... 하고 싶은 마음이 들다.

10) the sound (being) no more of an interruption than a consistent rain. 분사 구문. 내포된 접속사는 for 혹은 as, because. 마치 빗소리가 별로 신경 쓰이지 않듯이, 제리의 규칙적인 장작패는 소리도 신경에 거슬리지 않았다. no more... than...

"Anything is all right."

We went together back of the cabin. An astonishing amount of solid wood had been cut. There were cherry logs and heavy roots of rhododendron, and blocks from the waste pine and oak left from the building of the cabin.[11]

"But you've done as much as a man." I said, "This is a splendid pile."

I looked at him, actually for the first time. His hair was the color of the corn shocks and his eyes, very direct, were like the mountain sky when rain is pending ____ gray with a shadowing of that miraculous blue. As I spoke, a light came over him, as though the setting sun had touched him with the same suffused glory with which it touched the mountains. I gave him a quarter.

"You may come tomorrow" I said, "and thank you very much."

He looked at me, and at the coin, and seemed to want to speak, but could not, and turned away.

"I'll split kindling tomorrow" he said over his thin ragged shoulder. "You'll need kindling and medium wood[12] and logs and backlogs."

---

11) blocks from the waste pine and oak left from the building of the cabin. left는 앞의 oak를 수식하는 과거분사. 버려진 소나무나 집 지으면서 남겨진 떡갈나무를 가지고 만든 block. (나무를 벽돌처럼 반듯이 잘라놓은 모양을 의미)

12) He found a cubbyhole beside the fireplace that I had not noticed. There, of his own accord, he put kindling and medium wood. 제리는 내가 미처 못 봤던 벽난로 옆의 움푹 들어간 곳을 발견해내었다. 그리고는 그곳에, 자발적으로(of one's own accord), 불쏘시개용 나무와 중간크기 나무를 갖다 넣었다.

II

At daylight I was half wakened by the sound of chopping. Again it was so even in texture that I went back to sleep. When I left my bed in the cool morning, the boy had come and gone, and a stack of kindling was neat against the cabin wall. He came again after school in the afternoon and worked until time to return to the orphanage. His name was Jerry; he was twelve years old, and he had been at the orphanage since he was four. I could picture him at four, with the same grave gray-blue eyes and the same independence. No, the word that comes to me is "integrity."

The word means something very special to me, and the quality for which I use it is a rare one. My father had it __ there is another of whom I am almost sure __ but almost no man of my acquaintance possesses it with the clarity, the purity, the simplicity of a mountain stream. But the boy Jerry had it. It is bedded on courage, but it is more than brave. It is honest, but it is more than honesty. The ax handle broke one day, Jerry said the woodshop at the orphanage would repair it. I brought money to pay for the job and he refused it.

"I'll pay for it." he said. "I broke it. I brought the ax down careless."

"But no one hits accurately every time." I told him. "The fault was in the wood of the handle. I'll see the man from whom

I bought it."

It was only then that he would take the money, He was standing back of his own carelessness. He was a free-will agent and he chose to do careful work, and if he failed, he took the responsibility without subterfuge.

And he did for me the unnecessary thing, the gracious thing, that we find done only by the great of heart.[13] Things no training can teach, for they are done on the instant,[14] with no predicated experience. He found a cubbyhole beside the fireplace that I had not noticed. There, of his own accord, he put kindling and "medium" wood, so that I might always have dry fire material ready in case of sudden wet weather. A stone was loose in the rough walk to the cabin. He dug a deeper hole and steadied it, although he came, himself, by a short cut over the bank.[15] I found that when I tried to return his thoughtfulness with such things as candy and apples, he was wordless. "Thank you" was, perhaps, an expression for which he had had no use,

---

13) he did for me the unnecessary thing, the gracious thing, that we find done only by the great of heart. that은 관계대명사. 제리는 나를 위해 하지 않아도 되는 일, 은혜로운 일들을 해주었다. 그런 일은 단지 마음의 위대함(위대한 마음)으로서만 된다는 것을 우리는 안다.

14) Things no training can teach, for they are done on the instant. Things 다음에 관계대 명사 that 생략. 그 어떤 연습도 가르쳐 줄 수 없는 것들, 왜냐하면 그런 것들은 순간적으로 행해 지는 것이기 때문에.

15) A stone was loose in the rough walk to the cabin. He dug a deeper hole and steadied it, although he came, himself, by a short cut over the bank. 집으로 이르는 대강 만든 보도(널찍한 돌 같은 것을 드문드문 박아 놓은 길)에 한 돌이 헐거워졌다. 그러면 제리는 더 깊은 구멍을 판 뒤, 그 돌을 고정시켰다. 자신은 언덕 너머로 난 지름길로 다녔음에도 불구하고.

for his courtesy was instinctive. He only looked at the gift and at me, and a curtain lifted, so that I saw deep into the clear well of his eyes, and gratitude was there, and affection, soft over the firm granite of his character.

He made simple excuses to come and sit with me. I could no more have turned him away than if he had been physically hungry.16) I suggested once that the best time for us to visit was just before supper, when I left off my writing. After that, he waited always until my typewriter had been some time quiet. One day I worked until nearly dark. I went outside the cabin, having forgotten him. I saw him going up over the hill in the twilight toward the orphanage. When I sat down on fly stoop, a place was warm from his body where he had been sitting.

He became intimate, of course, with my pointer Pat. There is a strange communion between a boy and a dog. Perhaps they possess the same singleness of spirit, the same kind of wisdom. It is difficult to explain, but it exists. When I went across the state for a week end, I left the dog in Jerry's charge. I gave him the dog whistle and the key to the cabin, and left sufficient food. He was to come two or three times a day and let out the dog, and feed and exercise him. I should return Sunday night, and

---

16) He made simple excuses to come and sit with me. I could no more have turned him away than if he had been physically hungry. 제리는 나에게 와서 옆에 앉을 수 있도록 소박한 핑계를 만들어냈다. 나는 제리가 육체적으로 굶주렸을 때 (그를 모른 채 할 수 없듯이) (그렇게 핑계를 대면서 내 곁에 있으려고 하는) 제리를 모른 채 돌려보낼 수가 없었다.

Jerry would take out the dog for the last time Sunday afternoon and then leave the key under an agreed hiding place.

My return was belated and fog filled the mountain passes so treacherously that I dared not drive at night.[17] The fog held the next morning, and it was Monday noon before I reached the cabin. The dog had been fed and cared for that morning. Jerry came early in the afternoon, anxious.

"The superintendent said nobody would drive in the fog." he said. "I came just before bedtime last night and you hadn't come. So I brought Pat some of my breakfast this morning. I wouldn't have let anything happen to him."

"I was sure of that. I didn't worry."

"When I heard about the fog, I thought you'd know."

He was needed for work at the orphanage and he had to return at once. I gave him a dollar in payment, and he looked at it and went away. But that night he came in the darkness and knocked at the door.

"Come in, Jerry;" I said, "if you're allowed to be away this late."

"I told maybe a story;" he said. "I told them I thought you would want to see me."

"That's true." I assured him, and I saw his relief. "I want to hear about how you managed with the dog."

---

17) My return was belated and fog filled the mountain passes so treacherously that I dared not drive at night. 나의 귀가는 늦어졌다. 게다가 안개가 산길에 위험스럽게 가득했기 때문에 나는 야간 운전을 할 수가 없었다.

He sat by the fire with me, with no other light, and told me of their two days together. The dog lay close to him, and found a comfort there that I did not have for him. And it seemed to me that being with my dog, and caring for him, had brought the boy and me, too, together, so that he felt that he belonged to me as well as to the animal.

"He stayed right with me." he told me, "except when he ran in the laurel. He likes the laurel. I took him up over the hill and we both ran fast. There was a place where the grass was high and I lay down in it and hid. I could hear Pat hunting for me. He found my trail and he barked. When he found me, he acted crazy and he ran around and around me, in circles."

We watched the flames.

"That's an apple log." he said. "It burns the prettiest of any wood."

We were very close.

He was suddenly impelled to speak of things he had not spoken of before, nor had I cared to ask him.

"You look a little bit like my mother." he said. "Especially in the dark, by the fire."

"But you were only four, Jerry, when you came here. You have remembered how she looked, all these years?"

"My mother lives in Mannville." he said.

For a moment, finding that he had a mother shocked me as greatly as anything in my life has ever done, and I did not know why it disturbed me. Then I understood my distress. I was filled with a passionate resentment that any woman should go away and leave her son. A fresh anger added itself. The orphanage was a wholesome place, the executives were kind, good people, the food was more than adequate, the boys were healthy, a ragged shirt was no hardship, nor the doing of clean labor. Granted, perhaps, that the boy felt no lack, what blood fed the bowels of a woman who did not yearn over this child's lean body that had come in parturition out of her own?[18]

"Have you seen her, Jerry __ lately?"

"I see her every summer. She sends for me."

I wanted to cry out, "Why are you not with her? How she let you go away again?"

He said, "She comes up here from Mannville whenever she can. She doesn't have a job now."

His face shone in the firelight.

---

18) A son like this one___ 이 부분은 화자가 너무 흥분하여 비논리적으로 발언하는 부분임. A son like this one___ The orphanage was a wholesome place, the executives were kind, good people, the food was more than adequate, the boys were healthy, a ragged shirt was no hardship, nor the doing of clean labor. Granted, perhaps, that the boy felt no lack, what blood fed the bowels of a woman who did not yearn over this child's lean body that had come in parturition out of her own? 이런 아들을... (물론) 보육원은 위생적인 곳이고, 운영하는 사람들도 친절하고 좋은 사람들이었다. 음식 또한 보통 이상이었으며, 아이들은 건강했다. 낡은 셔츠가 꼭 고난은 아니며, 청소일 또한 고난이 아니다. (그래서) 제리가 아무 부족함을 못 느낀다 치자. 하지만 자기 몸에서 나온 이 아이의 여린 몸을 그리워하지 않는 여성의 배 속에는 어떤 피가 흐르는가? Granted that... that 이하를 인정한다 하여도. come in parturition 출산하다.

"She wanted to give me a puppy but they can't let any one boy keep a puppy. You remember the suit I had on last Sunday?" He was plainly proud. "She sent me that for Christmas. The Christmas before that" __ he drew a long breath, savoring the memory __ "she sent me a pair of skates."

"Roller skates?"

My mind was busy making pictures of her, trying to understand her. She had not, then, entirely deserted or forgotten him. But why then __ I thought, "I must not condemn her without knowing."

"Roller skates. I let the other boys use them. They're always borrowing them. But they're careful of them."

What circumstance other than poverty __

"I'm going to take the dollar you gave me for taking care of Pat." he said, "and buy her a pair of gloves."

I could only say "That will be nice. Do you know her size?"

"I think it's 8 1/2." he said.

He looked at my hands.

"Do you wear 8 1/2?" he asked.

"No. wear a smaller size, a 6."

"Oh! Then I guess her hands are bigger than yours."

I hated her. Poverty or no, there was other food than bread, and the soul could starve as quickly as the body. He was taking his dollar to buy gloves for her big stupid hands, and she lived away from him, in Mannville, and contented herself with sending him skates.

"She likes white gloves." he said. "Do you think I can get them for a dollar?"

"I think so." I said.

I decided that I should not leave the mountains without seeing her and knowing for myself why she had done this thing.

III

The human mind scatters its interests as though made of thistledown, and every wind stirs and moves it.[19] I finished my work. It did not please me, and I gave my thoughts to another field. I should need some Mexican material.

I made arrangements to close my Florida place. Mexico immediately and doing the writing there, if conditions were favorable. Then, Alaska with my brother. After that, heaven knew what or where.

I did not take time to go to Mannville to see Jerry's mother, nor even to talk with the orphanage officials about her. I was a trifle abstracted about the boy; because of my work and

---

19) The human mind scatters its interests as though made of thistledown, and every wind stirs and moves it. 인간의 마음은 마치 엉겅퀴꽃처럼(불면 후루루 날아가는) 그 관심사를 흐트러뜨린다. 이런 저런 바람이 흔들어 그 마음을 날려버린다.

plans. And after my first fury at her __ we did not speak of her again __ his having a mothers any sort at all, not far away in Mannville, relieved me of the ache I had had about him. He did not question the anomalous relation. He was not lonely, It was none of my concern.

He came every day and cut my wood and did small helpful favors and stayed to talk. The days had become cold, and often I let him come inside the cabin. He would lie on the floor in front of the fire, with one arm across the pointer, and they would both doze and wait quietly for me. Other days they ran with a common ecstasy through the laurel, and since the asters were now gone, he brought me back vermilion maple leaves, and chestnut boughs dripping with imperial yellow. I was ready to go.

I said to him, "You have been my good friend, Jerry, I shall often think of you and miss you. Pat will miss you too. I am leaving tomorrow."

He did not answer. When he went away I remember that a new moon hung over the mountains, and I watched him go in silence up the hill. I expected him the next day; but he did not come. The details of packing my personal belongings, loading my car, arranging the bed over the seat, where the dog would ride, occupied me until late in the day, I closed the cabin and started the car, noticing that the sun was in the west and I should do well to be out of the mountains by nightfall.

I stopped by the orphanage and left the cabin key and money for my light bill with Miss Clark.

"And will you call Jerry for me to say good-by to him?"

"I don't know where he is." she said. "I'm afraid he's not well. He didn't eat his dinner this noon. One of the other boys saw him going over the hill into the laurel. He was supposed to fire the boiler this afternoon. It's not like him; he's unusually reliable."

I was almost relieved, for I knew I should never see him again, and it would be easier not to say good-by to him.

I said, "I wanted to talk with you about his mother __ why he's here __ but I'm in more of a hurry than I expected to be. It's out of the question for me to see her now, too. But here's some money I'd like to leave with you to buy things for him at Christmas and on his birthday, It will be better than for me to try to send him things. I could so easily duplicate __ skates, for instance."

She blinked her honest spinster's eyes.

"There's not much use for skates here." she said.

Her stupidity annoyed me.

"What I mean." I said, "is that I don't want to duplicate skates his mother sends him. I might have chosen skates if I didn't know she had already given them to him."

She stared at me.

"I don't understand." she said. "He has no mother. He has no skates."

Comprehension Check-Up Questions

1. Describe how bitter winter is in the orphanage.

2. For what did the narrator come to the Carolina mountains?

3. What brought Jerry to the narrator's?

4. Describe Jerry when the narrator first saw him.

5. Why did the narrator want to pay Jerry for his job immediately on the day?

6. How well did Jerry do his job?

7. Why did the narrator look at Jerry with new eyes and how did he appear at this time?

8. Why did the narrator pay Jerry a quarter instead of a dime?

9. How was the sound of Jerry's chopping and what does this tell about it?

10. What suggests Jerry's diligence and responsibility?

11. Why did the narrator put Pat under Jerry's care?

12. When was she supposed to return and when did she actually do? What made such delay?

13. What did Jerry's two-day company with Pat result in?

14. Why did the narrator decide to leave Carolina and whereto would she go?

15. Why didn't leaving Jerry hurt her so much as expected?

16. In what season did she leave the mountain? Then how long had she stayed there approximately?

17. How did Jerry respond to the news that she would leave?

18. Why couldn't she see Jerry when she last visited the orphanage?

The Landlady

Roald Dahl

Roald Dahl (/'roʊ.əld 'dɑːl/;1916 −1990) was a British novelist, short story writer, poet, screenwriter, and fighter pilot. His books have sold more than 250 million copies worldwide. Born in Wales to Norwegian immigrant parents, Dahl served in the Royal Air Force during the Second World War. He became a flying ace and intelligence officer, rising to the rank of acting wing commander. He rose to prominence as a writer in the 1940s with works for both children and adults, and he became one of the world's best-selling authors. He has been referred to as "one of the greatest storytellers for children of the 20th century". Dahl's short stories are known for their unexpected endings, and his children's books for their unsentimental, macabre, often darkly comic mood, featuring villainous adult enemies of the child characters. Dahl's works for children include *James and the Giant Peach, Charlie and the Chocolate Factory, Matilda, The Witches, Fantastic Mr Fox, The BFG, The Twits and George's Marvellous Medicine*. His adult works include *Tales of the Unexpected*.

reading

bath

station entrance

like a flat blade of ice

a fairly cheap hotel

the porter

quarter-mile

the branch manager

briskly

identical

very swanky residences

white facades

cracked and blotchy

a printed notice

the hearth

unpack

ground floor

off her rocker

trotted downstairs

the guest book

dachshund

was curled up asleep

with its nose tucked

into its belly

pretty decent house

a pub

a boardinghouse

conjured up

rapacious landladies

kippers

dame

a jack-in-the-box

be simply swamped

with applicants

just a teeny-weeny bit

choosy and particular

a hot-water bottle

rings a bell

tantalizing

a whiff of a peculiar smell

masses of fillings

I

Billy Weaver had traveled down from London on the slow afternoon train, with a change at Reading on the way, and by the time he got to Bath, it was about nine o'clock in the evening, and the moon was coming up out of a clear starry sky over the houses opposite the station entrance. But the air was deadly cold and the wind was like a flat blade of ice on his cheeks.

"Excuse me." he said, "but is there a fairly cheap hotel not too far away from here?"

"Try The Bell and Dragon." the porter answered, pointing down the road. "They might take you in. It's about a quarter of a mile along on the other side."

Billy thanked him and picked up his suitcase and set out to walk the quarter-mile to The Bell and Dragon. He had never been to Bath before. He didn't know anyone who lived there. But Mr. Greenslade at the head office in London had told him it was a splendid town. "Find your own lodgings." he had said, "and then go along and report to the branch manager as soon as you've got yourself settled."

Billy was seventeen years old. He was wearing a new navy-blue overcoat, a new brown trilby hat, and a new brown suit, and he was feeling fine. He walked briskly down the street. He was trying to do everything briskly these days. Briskness, he had decided, was the one common characteristic of all successful businessmen. The big shots up at the head office were absolutely fantastically brisk all the time. They were amazing.

There were no shops on this wide street that he was walking along, only a line of tall houses on each side, all of them identical. They had porches and pillars and four or five steps going up to their front doors, and it was obvious that once upon a time they had been very swanky residences. But now, even in the darkness, he could see that the paint was peeling from the woodwork on their doors and windows and that the handsome white facades were cracked and blotchy from neglect.

Suddenly, in a downstairs window that was brilliantly illuminated by a street lamp not six yards away, Billy caught sight of a printed notice propped up against the glass in one of the upper panes. It said BED AND BREAKFAST. There was a vase of yellow chrysanthemums, tall and beautiful, standing just underneath the notice.

He stopped walking. He moved a bit closer. Green curtains (some sort of velvety material) were hanging down on either side of the window. The chrysanthemums looked wonderful beside them. He went right up and peered through the glass into the room, and the first thing he saw was a bright fire burning in the hearth. On the carpet in front of the fire, a pretty little dachshund was curled up asleep with its nose tucked into its belly.[1] The room itself, so far as he could see in the half darkness, was filled with pleasant furniture. There was a baby grand piano and a big sofa and several plump armchairs, and in one corner he spotted a large parrot in a cage. Animals were usually a good sign in a place like this, Billy told himself; and all in all, it looked to him as though it would be a pretty decent house to stay in. Certainly it would be more comfortable than The Bell and Dragon.

On the other hand, a pub would be more congenial than a boardinghouse. There would be beer and darts in the evenings, and lots of people to talk to, and it would probably be a good bit cheaper, too. He had stayed a couple of nights in a pub once before and he had liked it. He had never stayed in any boardinghouses, and, to be perfectly honest, he was a tiny bit frightened of them. The name itself conjured up images of watery cabbage, rapacious landladies, and a powerful smell of kippers in the living room.[2]

After dithering about like this in the cold for two or three minutes, Billy decided that he would walk on and take a look at The Bell and Dragon before making up his mind. He turned to go.

---

1) 배에 코를 파묻은 채.
2) 보디아우스라는 단어 자체가 흐물거리는 양배추, 탐욕슬운 여주인, 거실에 강하게 남아 있는 훈제 청어 냄새 등의 이미지를 떠올렸다.

And now a queer thing happened to him. He was in the act of stepping back and turning away from the window when all at once his eye was caught and held in the most peculiar manner by the small notice that was there. BED AND BREAKFAST, it said. BED AND BREAKFAST, BED AND BREAKFAST, BED AND BREAKFAST. Each word was like a large black eye staring at him through the glass, holding him, compelling him, forcing him to stay where he was and not to walk away from that house, and the next thing he knew, he was actually moving across from the window to the front door of the house, climbing the steps that led up to it, and reaching for the bell.[3]

II

He pressed the bell. Far away in a back room he heard it ringing, and then at once — it must have been at once because he hadn't even had time to take his finger from the bell button— the door swung open and a woman was standing there.[4] Normally you ring the bell and you have at least a half-minute's wait before the door opens. But this dame was like a jack-in-the-box. He pressed the bell — and out she popped! It made him jump.

---

3) 현관벨로 손을 뻗치고 있었다.
4) 그러자 동시에 _ 동시에 라고 할 수 밖에 없는 것이 왜냐하면 그가 미처 벨버튼에서 손을 뗄 시간도 없었기 때문에 _ 현관문이 활짝 열리면서 여자가 서 있었다.

She was about forty-five or fifty years old, and the moment she saw him, she gave him a warm, welcoming smile.

" Please come in." she said pleasantly. She stepped aside, holding the door wide open, and Billy found himself automatically starting forward. The compulsion or, more accurately, the desire to follow after her into that house was extraordinarily strong.

"I saw the notice in the window." he said, holding himself back.5)

"Yes, I know."

"I was wondering about a room."

"It's all ready for you, my dear." she said. She had a round pink face and very gentle blue eyes.

"I was on my way to The Bell and Dragon." Billy told her. "But the notice in your window just happened to catch my eye."

"My dear boy." she said, "why don't you come in out of the cold?"

"How much do you charge?"

"Five and sixpence a night, including breakfast."

It was fantastically cheap. It was less than half of what he had been willing to pay.

"If that is too much." she added, "then perhaps I can reduce it just a tiny bit. Do you desire an egg for breakfast? Eggs are expensive

5) 자신(의 기쁜 마음)을 억제하면서.

at the moment. It would be sixpence less without the egg."

"Five and sixpence is fine." he answered. "I should like very much to stay here."

"I knew you would. Do come in."

She seemed terribly nice. She looked exactly like the mother of one's best school friend welcoming one into the house to stay for the Christmas holidays. Billy took off his hat and stepped over the threshold.

"Just hang it there." she said, "and let me help you with your coat."

There were no other hats or coats in the hall. There were no umbrellas, no walking sticks—nothing.

"We have it all to ourselves."[6] she said, smiling at him over her shoulder as she led the way upstairs. "You see, it isn't very often I have the pleasure of taking a visitor into my little nest."[7]

The old girl is slightly dotty, Billy told himself. But at five and sixpence a night, who cares about that? "I should've thought you'd be simply swamped with applicants."[8] he said politely.

"Oh, I am, my dear, I am, of course I am. But the trouble is that I'm inclined to be just a teeny-weeny bit choosy and particular[9]—if you see what I mean."

---

6) 우리 둘 밖에 없다.

7) 우리의 작은 둥지: boardinghouse를 가리킴.

8) 당신 boardinghouse가 고객으로 만원일 것이다.

9) 약간 까다롭고 특별한 것을 좋아한다. a teeny-weeny bit = a little bit.

"Ah, yes."

"But I'm always ready. Everything is always ready day and night in this house just on the off chance that an acceptable young gentleman will come along.10) And it is such a pleasure, my dear, such a very great pleasure when now and again I open the door and I see someone standing there who is just exactly right." She was halfway up the stairs,11) and she paused with one hand on the stair rail, turning her head and smiling down at him with pale lips. "Like you." she added, and her blue eyes traveled slowly all the way down the length of Billy's body, to his feet, and then up again.

On the second-floor landing she said to him, "This floor is mine."

They climbed up another flight. "And this one is all yours." she said. "Here's your room. I do hope you'll like it." She took him into a small but charming front bedroom, switching on the light as she went in.

"The morning sun comes right in the window, Mr. Perkins. It is Mr. Perkins, isn't it?"

"No." he said. "It's Weaver."

"Mr. Weaver. How nice. I've put a water bottle between the sheets to air them out,12) Mr. Weaver. It's such a comfort to have

---

10) 괜찮은 젊은이가 올 경우를 대비하여.
11) 계단을 반쯤 올라가 있는 상태.
12) 침대시트 (눅눅한) 공기를 날려버리기 위해 뜨거운 물병을 넣어두었다. 난방시설이 부실한 영국에

a hot-water bottle in a strange bed with clean sheets, don't you agree? And you may light the gas fire at any time if you feel chilly."

"Thank you." Billy said. "Thank you ever so much." He noticed that the bedspread had been taken off the bed and that the bedclothes had been neatly turned back on one side, all ready for someone to get in.

"I'm so glad you appeared." she said, looking earnestly into his face. "I was beginning to get worried."

"That's all right." Billy answered brightly. "You mustn't worry about me." He put his suitcase on the chair and started to open it.

"And what about supper, my dear? Did you manage to get anything to eat before you came here?"

"I'm not a bit hungry, thank you." he said. "I think I'll just go to bed as soon as possible because tomorrow I've got to get up rather early and report to the office."

"Very well, then. I'll leave you now so that you can unpack. But before you go to bed, would you be kind enough to pop into the sitting room on the ground floor and sign the book?13) Everyone has to do that because it's the law of the land, and we don't want to go breaking any laws at this stage in the proceedings, do we?" She gave him a little wave of the hand and went quickly out of the room and closed the door.

서 일반적으로 사용했던 방법임.

13) 1층 거실로 내려와 방명록에 사인하다.

Now, the fact that his landlady appeared to be slightly off her rocker[14] didn't worry Billy in the least. After all, she not only was harmless — there was no question about that — but she was also quite obviously a kind and generous soul. He guessed that she had probably lost a son in the war, or something like that, and had never gotten over it.

III

So a few minutes later, after unpacking his suitcase and washing his hands, he trotted downstairs to the ground floor[15] and entered the living room. His landlady wasn't there, but the fire was glowing in the hearth, and the little dachshund was still sleeping soundly in front of it. The room was wonderfully warm and cozy. I'm a lucky fellow, he thought, rubbing his hands. This is a bit of all right.

He found the guest book lying open on the piano, so he took out his pen and wrote down his name and address. There were only two other entries above his on the page,[16] and as one always does with guest books, he started to read them. One was a Christopher Mulholland from Cardiff. The other was Gregory

---

14) 약간 정신이 이상하다는 사실. off her rocker: insane.
15) 계단을 총총 내려 1층으로 내려갔다.
16) 방명록 페이지를 보니 2개의 다른 사람 이름만이 자기 이름 위에 있었다.

W. Temple from Bristol.

That's funny, he thought suddenly. Christopher Mulholland. It rings a bell.[17)]

Now where on earth had he heard that rather unusual name before?

Was it a boy at school? No. Was it one of his sister's numerous young men, perhaps, or a friend of his father's? No, no, it wasn't any of those. He glanced down again at the book.

Christopher Mulholland
231 Cathedral Road, Cardiff

Gregory W. Temple
27 Sycamore Drive, Bristol

As a matter of fact, now he came to think of it, he wasn't at all sure that the second name didn't have almost as much of a familiar ring about it as the first.[18)]

"Gregory Temple?" he said aloud, searching his memory. "Christopher Mulholland?..."

"Such charming boys." a voice behind him answered, and he turned and saw his landlady sailing into the room[19)] with a

---

17) 뭔가 기억을 떠올리게 하다.
18) 두 번째 이름도 첫 번째 이름만큼 귀에 익었다.
19) 마치 돛배처럼 부드럽게 방으로 들어오는. sailing 이하는 saw의 보어.

large silver tea tray in her hands. She was holding it well out in front of her, and rather high up, as though the tray were a pair of reins on a frisky horse.[20]

"They sound somehow familiar." he said.

"They do? How interesting."

"I'm almost positive I've heard those names before somewhere. Isn't that odd?

Maybe it was in the newspapers. They weren't famous in any way, were they? I mean famous cricketers or footballers or something like that?"

"Famous." she said, setting the tea tray down on the low table in front of the sofa. "Oh no, I don't think they were famous. But they were incredibly handsome, both of them, I can promise you that. They were tall and young and handsome, my dear, just exactly like you."

Once more, Billy glanced down at the book. "Look here." he said, noticing the dates. "This last entry is over two years old."

"It is?"

"Yes, indeed. And Christopher Mulholland's is nearly a year before that — more than three years ago."

"Dear me." she said, shaking her head and heaving a dainty little sigh.[21] "I would never have thought it. How time does fly

---

20) 마치 활기찬 말에 매어 둔 한 쌍의 말고삐인 듯이 쟁반을 높이 들고 옴.
21) 작은 한숨을 쉬면서.

away from us all, doesn't it, Mr. Wilkins?"

"It's Weaver." Billy said. "W-e-a-v-e-r."

"Oh, of course it is!" she cried, sitting down on the sofa. "How silly of me. I do apologize. In one ear and out the other,[22] that's me, Mr. Weaver."

"You know something?" Billy said. "Something that's really quite extraordinary about all this?"

"No, dear, I don't."

"Well, you see, both of these names __ Mulholland and Temple __ I not only seem to remember each one of them separately, so to speak, but somehow or other, in some peculiar way, they both appear to be sort of connected together as well. As though they were both famous for the same sort of thing, if you see what I mean __ like... well... like Dempsey and Tunney, for example, or Churchill and Roosevelt."

"How amusing." she said. "But come over here now, dear, and sit down beside me on the sofa and I'll give you a nice cup of tea and a ginger biscuit before you go to bed."

"You really shouldn't bother." Billy said. "I didn't mean you to do anything like that." He stood by the piano, watching her as she fussed about with the cups and saucers. He noticed that she had small, white, quickly moving hands and red fingernails.

"I'm almost positive it was in the newspapers I saw them."

---

22) 한 귀로 들어와서는 즉시 다른 귀로 나간다. 금방 잊어버린다.

Billy said. "I'll think of it in a second. I'm sure I will."

There is nothing more tantalizing than a thing like this that lingers just outside the borders of one's memory. He hated to give up.

"Now wait a minute." he said. "Wait just a minute. Mulholland... Christopher Mulholland... wasn't that the name of the Eton schoolboy who was on a walking tour through the West Country, and then all of a sudden..."

"Milk?" she said. "And sugar?"

"Yes, please. And then all of a sudden..."

"Eton schoolboy?" she said. "Oh no, my dear, that can't possibly be right, because my Mr. Mulholland was certainly not an Eton schoolboy when he came to me. He was a Cambridge undergraduate. Come over here now and sit next to me and warm yourself in front of this lovely fire. Come on. Your tea's all ready for you." She patted the empty place beside her on the sofa, and she sat there smiling at Billy and waiting for him to come over.

He crossed the room slowly and sat down on the edge of the sofa. She placed his teacup on the table in front of him.

"There we are." she said. "How nice and cozy this is, isn't it?"

IV

Billy started sipping his tea. She did the same. For half a minute or so, neither of them spoke. But Billy knew that she was looking at him. Her body was half turned toward him, and he could feel her eyes resting on his face, watching him over the rim of her teacup. Now and again, he caught a whiff of a peculiar smell that seemed to emanate directly from her person. It was not in the least unpleasant, and it reminded him __ well, he wasn't quite sure what it reminded him of. Pickled walnuts? New leather? Or was it the corridors of a hospital?

At length, she said, "Mr. Mulholland was a great one for his tea. Never in my life have I seen anyone drink as much tea as dear, sweet Mr. Mulholland."

"I suppose he left fairly recently." Billy said. He was still puzzling his head about the two names. He was positive now that he had seen them in the newspapers __ in the headlines.

"Left?" she said, arching her brows. "But my dear boy, he never left. He's still here. Mr. Temple is also here. They're on the fourth floor, both of them together."

Billy set his cup down slowly on the table and stared at his landlady. She smiled back at him, and then she put out one of her white hands and patted him comfortingly on the knee. "How old are you, my dear?" she asked.

"Seventeen."

"Seventeen!" she cried. "Oh, it's the perfect age! Mr. Mulholland was also seventeen. But I think he was a trifle shorter than you are; in fact I'm sure he was, and his teeth weren't quite so white. You have the most beautiful teeth, Mr. Weaver, did you know that?"

"They're not as good as they look." Billy said. "They've got simply masses of fillings in them at the back."

"Mr. Temple, of course, was a little older." she said, ignoring his remark. "He was actually twenty-eight. And yet I never would have guessed it if he hadn't told me, never in my whole life. There wasn't a blemish on his body."

"A what?" Billy said.

"His skin was just like a baby's."

There was a pause. Billy picked up his teacup and took another sip of his tea; then he set it down again gently in its saucer. He waited for her to say something else, but she seemed to have lapsed into another of her silences. He sat there staring straight ahead of him into the far corner of the room, biting his lower lip.

"That parrot." he said at last. "You know something? It had me completely fooled when I first saw it through the window. I could have sworn it was alive."

"Alas, no longer."

"It's most terribly clever the way it's been done." he said. "It doesn't look in the least bit dead. Who did it?"

"I did."

"You did?"

"Of course." she said. "And have you met my little Basil as well?" She nodded toward the dachshund curled up so comfortably in front of the fire. Billy looked at it. And suddenly, he realized that this animal had all the time been just as silent and motionless as the parrot. He put out a hand and touched it gently on the top of its back. The back was hard and cold, and when he pushed the hair to one side with his fingers, he could see the skin underneath, grayish black and dry and perfectly preserved.

"Good gracious me." he said. "How absolutely fascinating." He turned away from the dog and stared with deep admiration at the little woman beside him on the sofa. "It must be most awfully difficult to do a thing like that."

"Not in the least." she said. "I stuff all my little pets myself when they pass away. Will you have another cup of tea?"

"No, thank you." Billy said. The tea tasted faintly of bitter almonds, and he didn't much care for it.

"You did sign the book, didn't you?"

"Oh, yes."

"That's good. Because later on, if I happen to forget what

you were called, then I could always come down here and look it up. I still do that almost every day with Mr. Mulholland and Mr.... Mr...."

"Temple." Billy said, "Gregory Temple. Excuse my asking, but haven't there been any other guests here except them in the last two or three years?"

Holding her teacup high in one hand, inclining her head slightly to the left, she looked up at him out of the corners of her eyes and gave him another gentle little smile.

"No, my dear." she said. "Only you."

1. What aspects of the house make Billy feel it would be a good place to stay?

2. What evidence is there that the landlady had been expecting a guest?

3. What are the first signs that the landlady is very odd?

4. Billy doesn't finish his sentence about Christopher Mulholland. What was he about to say?

5. What is frightening when the landlady says Mr. Temple had perfect skin "just like a baby's"?

6. Do you think Billy will die? Explain why you think so.